Preface

One day I found myself in a strange scenario. I was laying on the floor, wadded up into the fetal position on the floor next to my bed. I was looking at the dust bunnies and array of forgotten items under there.

I had a mind full of persistent dark worries, dogging along everywhere I went. I felt like I had waded out into a pool of thick, dark tar. Every direction I went, the pool only got deeper. I tried to run but could only squirm. I tried to scream but could only sigh.

In the other room, on the kitchen counter sat a foreclosure notice. Underneath that, shut of notices from 3 different utilities. I had no job. No prospects for a new job. I had been sending out my résumé for anything I qualified for or didn't. There wasn't so much as a glimmer, sparkle, or sliver of hope in my life at that moment.

I wadded up all this emotion and heaped it up in a babble of a prayer.

"Now hold up" I can hear you muttering. "What does this all have to do with anything?"

Well… everything. If you would calm down and stop asking so many questions, then we could all get on with this story of mine.

Now, where was I? Right. Prayer. I have a hard time believing that all life formed by happenchance. Some anomaly that was somehow propagated by accident. Every natural system that I know of deteriorates, degrades and atrophies over time.

Somehow our solar system came to be? Everything lined up exactly? The Earth was able to buck the system, evolve, and develop into the amazing system that it is? No. I'm not buying it.

There was a hand in this process. I believe in a higher intellect. A supreme being. This human experience for us. There are many names for this deity, but we are all talking about the same thing. Because he cares for us, and created everything around us, I thought he could give me some direction.

The best way I know how to seek after that direction is by addressing deity specifically through a prayer. Which I did.

The way we hear back is, somewhat of an individual experience. I have spoken with many people that have felt his presence. Most describe something a little different. The common themes are an inner warmth. Feelings of peace, calm, serenity or comfort.

Immediately following my prayer, I felt calm. I felt a warmth that started with a tingling sensation on my head and spread through my body. Though the words came as a whisper, they were distinct and clear. "Be Grateful".

My initial reaction was almost indignant. "For what?" I knew there was some depth to those words, but my sense of humor briefly mused over them. "Could there be more counter-intuitive, backwards advice possible?"

As I analyzed, implemented, and metabolized that message. I realized how relevant and concise it was.

I challenge you to take a few moments to think about the first thing your eyes rest on.

There might be a pencil on your desk. Have you ever thought about where the graphite came from for the pencil? What about the wood in the pencil? Do certain types of wood make better pencils? What about the router that shapes the pencil out of wood? What about the groove in the center of the pencil for the graphite? When is that cut?

There is already a lot of work that went into that pencil. It still needs glued, painted, an eraser, an aluminum ferrule. the ferrule still requires extrusion and crimped onto the pencil.

How do they paint the ferrule? Some pencils have the manufacturer, and type of pencil embossed into the pencil. Then then painted again. How is that done? What is the eraser made of? Who decided they should be pink? How do they give the erasers coloration? Who invented the eraser?

There are centuries of innovation and development in that one pencil. That pencil assembles from components all over the world. That pencil is miraculous. We don't even think about it. That's one tiny, insignificant item.

We are surrounded, covered and drenched in amazing things all around us. We don't take the time to consider any of it.

The natural evolution of this observation was amazement and gratitude. A childlike awe for the most ordinary items. In the following days, I found myself looking at ordinary objects as if I had never seen them before.

In college, I took an art class. We studied the book

"Drawing on the Right Side of the Brain". One of the chapters discussed a technique of redrawing a picture by turning it upside down.

We tried it as a class. Everyone in the class chose a picture and we tried to redraw the picture as we saw it. Some were better than others. But I would not say that any of the attempts looked very good. Then we flipped the picture that we were drawing upside down and redrew them again. It was magic. They all turned out near perfect.

We were not instructed how to draw any better between our first and second attempts. Why were we able to suddenly and miraculously redraw a picture?

When your brain sees an image that it is familiar with, such as a picture of an ear, it knows what an ear looks like. Unless you are trained. Unless you or the gift of fine detail observation. Your brain will glaze over most of the details, because our brains are lazy. Well, not lazy, but efficient. We all have limited bandwidth with our processing abilities. The brain will filter out the non-essential details.

DVD players and movie compression software do the exact same thing. A movie is nothing more than a series of images sequentially displayed. Usually 24 images per second. Pay attention the next time you are watching a movie. Most of what you are seeing, does not change. The background, for example is stationary. It is usually the actor that is moving.

Rather than redrawing everything over and over dozens of times per second. The DVD player will only update the portions of the movie that are moving or changing. Using complex algorithms, movie files are compressed, and files are reduced to a fraction of their original size. without much loss in image quality. Our mind will do the same thing with objects that are familiar.

In the 18th century there was a man with minimal education, named Michael Faraday. Michael worked for 7 years as an apprentice in a print shop making books. Being a curious person, he began reading the books as they were being printed. Several books inspired him, including Isaac Watts's *The Improvement of the Mind*. He also developed an interest in science, especially in electricity. Faraday was particularly inspired by the book *Conversations on Chemistry* by Jane Marcet.

With only an inquisitive mind and minimal education, Michael invented the following:

- Electromagnetic rotation
- Gas liquefaction and refrigeration
- Benzene
- Electromagnetic Induction
- Faraday effect (magneto optical effect)
- Diamagnetism
- The first electric motor and dynamo

Albert Einstein kept a picture of Michael in his office. That is how spectacular his accomplishments were.

Lacking knowledge on the matter, Michael plowed through one discovery after another. The only skill set he used was a rabid curiosity about the world around him.

I learned from that experience that gratitude begets awe. Awe begets amazement. Amazement begets curiosity. Curiosity helps you, and others discover answers to life's difficult challenges.

In this book, I try to take a fresh look at a puzzle that is fascinating to me. The challenge of marketing. Why do some inferior products rise to the top of their market? Why do some great products and industry standard products wither and die? Why do some brands develop cult like following? Why are some plagued with PR nightmares and poor public image? This is my attempt to take a look at it through the lens of my understanding.

New Frontiers

On July 11, 1897, a hydrogen balloon prepped for flight. The exploratory mission was leaving the shores of Svalbard Island near Norway.
At the time, Norway had fallen way behind in the race to place a group of explorers on the North Pole.
Amid cheering crowds, the adventurers Knut Fraenkel, Nils Strindberg, & S. A. Andrée bid family and friends goodbye.
As their balloon lofted into the air, Strindberg worried to this might be his last time seeing his fiancé.
Strindberg and Fraenkel had agreed to journey

with S.A. Andrée. He had the idea to travel to the North Pole by floating there effortlessly by balloon.

Andrée had experimented with several ideas to steer the balloon with sails. Undaunted, he pushed forward with his plans, despite having no idea how to get the balloon to the North Pole.

After a near crash on departure in front of the crowds, the Eagle managed to stay aloft for another 10 hours. Then began to bob and bump along the ground. The voyage continued on at this rate for 2 days, preventing any of the explorers from getting any sleep.

65 hours after launch, the balloon finally came to rest in the middle of the Arctic.

All three explorers were woefully inexperienced. None of them had the proper equipment to deal with the frigid conditions.

They decided to set off on foot for a cache of food that was only a few miles away. They then discovered that the drift of the ice fields was going in the opposite direction of their cache. Unfortunately, they were moving too slow through the jutting icescape. They were floating away from the cache faster than they could travel. they decided to alter course towards a second cache. This time fierce winds stopped their progress for the alternate cache. The three, weary and demoralized from lack of headway opted to set up camp on an ice floe and ride the ice South.

The travelers spent the rest of their time building an igloo and fending off frequent polar bear attacks.

As ice eventually does, it began to break up. They awoke one day to find their shelter disintegrating underneath them. With no remaining options the three took refuge on a passing island. For 33 years, their fate remained a mystery.

On August 5, 1930 a group of hunters discovered their remains, supplies, cameras and journals.

Their bodies returned to Sweden and given a hero's welcome.

Unfortunately, their bodies were cremated before autopsies could be performed. Little is known how they died.

In so many ways, the marketing landscape is a frozen expanse of uncharted territory that is constantly shifting and changing.

In this book we are taking a high-level look at marketing and the challenges that businesses face. The endlessly shifting landscape of marketing. We will dig into strategies that will help you chart out your path to your business goals. No more haphazardly floating your way to end-goals with little, to no idea how you can get there.

With new understanding, you will understand how to successfully bring products and services to market. You will experience repeatable your success,

The Problem with businesses

There is an expansive minefield businesses and owners navigate. Each of them trying to not harm or destroy their business. Some them are common sense, some we've heard about, and some we are completely unaware of.

There was a time in my life when I spent every single Friday evening slowly side shuffling through a Blockbuster Video store looking for a new movie to watch.

I can still remember the smell of a Blockbuster. They all smelled the same. A combination of buttered popcorn, electronics, a tiny kick of perfume/cologne, sprinkle in some fear and loneliness, and hint of unwashed hair. Why unwashed hair? I didn't make the rules up. This was Blockbuster, and that's how they smelled. There was always the uncertainty that they would have the movie you wanted. They had what seemed like 200 copies new releases. That still didn't guarantee that it would be available for rental.

Sometimes it felt like you won the lottery. The movie you were looking for would sometimes get returned by someone. You would see it sitting behind the counter there waiting to be put out on the shelves. You'd lean in to the person working behind the counter and whisper so that no one else heard "Hey… Hey! Can you hand me that movie that was just returned?" They would hand it to you, and then you'd nonchalantly walk over to your friends who were looking for another movie. Then you'd casually show the movie to them. They would all look at you like you were holding a Willy Wonka golden ticket.

That was the great parts about going to Blockbuster. It became a lot less great when you went up to the cash register. New releases were $2.99. Any other movie was $1.99. That's not too bad, right?

There were always late fees that you had accrued from your last rental. Oh, those fees! You always had fees. Your movie rental was for 24 hours. If you didn't get it back in 24 hours, it was $1 per day per video.

I was usually ambitious and would rent 3 movies. We usually only got through 1, sometimes 2 movies on Friday. Saturday night something usually came up and I wouldn't have time to watch the rest of the movies. Sunday I usually forgot. I'd usually remember the movies on Monday, watch them that night and return them by Tuesday.

It wasn't uncommon for my rental fees to be $6 for rental fees, and $12 in late fees; about what it cost to buy a new movie. Most everyone who left Blockbuster felt like they had become a victim of a robbery.

When Redbox came out, they offered movie rentals for $.99 per day. They had plenty of convenient places to return your movies. Places like at McDonalds, grocery stores and gas stations. Places where most people were going anyway.

At the same time Netflix arrived, and for $7.99 per month, anyone could rent as many movies as they wanted (one at a time). And they were mailed directly to your house. Everyone fled as fast as they could from Blockbuster, and never-ever went back.

Most of us didn't even feel bad when we saw Blockbuster after Blockbuster closing down. We didn't care if we never stepped into another Blockbuster again. Most of us had too many fees to go back anyway.

At the pinnacle of their operation, Blockbuster was the largest video rental business in the U.S.

10 years later, nearly out of business.

I have similar, rich memories at Sears and Kmart. I

got lost for my first time at Sears. I must have been about 4 years old. I couldn't understand how my mom could take so long shopping.

I am sure she wasn't that slow, but to a 4-year-old in the women's clothing section at the store? That was even more boring than church to me. And so -- to entertain myself, I began pushing through the clothes into the inner sanctum of the clothes racks. That was like being in a fort. That was great. I'd hang out there and watch the clothes move one by one as my mom slid the hangers and looked at each item, one at a time.

I liked to jump out between the clothes that she was looking at. Then, one of the times that I jumped out at her, I discovered, to my alarm that the woman I was trying to annoy was not my mom. In fact, my mom was nowhere around. I was completely panicked. I was way too shy to ask for help. I figured that I'd just have to live there. I'd probably end up dying of malnourishment one night. Alone. After everyone had gone home and locked up and turned out the lights. It was a shame. I had my whole life in front of me too.

I ended up wandering around for 2 or 3 hours… well, to me it felt like that long. It was more like 20 or 30 seconds. I don't even know if my mom knew I was missing.

And Kmart - talk about a place that had an iconic smell. Every Kmart everywhere always had the exact same smell. Smelled like cheap plastic.

Sears, Kmart, Blockbuster, just a few major retail stores that have all gone to the big strip mall in the sky. What happened?

In comparison, there is a handful of shiny, bright corporations that have risen to the top. Think of Apple, Amazon, Google and Facebook.

What kind of special mojo, or magic, or secret sauce knowledge do they have that the rest of us don't? Are they smarter than you and I will ever be? Maybe they got lucky? Are the Kmarts, Blockbusters, and Sears out their big idiots? Maybe they are unlucky?

Steve Jobs once said:

> "When you grow up you tend to get told the world is the way it is, and your life is just to live your life inside the world. Try not to bash into the walls too much. Try to have a nice family, have fun, save a little money. That's a very limited life. Life can be much broader once you discover one simple fact: Everything around you that you call life was made up by people that were no smarter than you and you can change it, you can influence it, you can build your own things that other people can use. Once you learn that, you'll never be the same again."

According to Steve Jobs, the people at Netflix are no smarter than the people at Blockbuster. They see the world through a different lens. They have a different understanding of how they can operate the world.

Both companies served the purpose of delivering movies to their customers. They both offered DVDs. Blockbuster offered VHS movies too. Blockbuster also let customers pick up movies locally and go home that day with their movie. Netflix sent you one movie at a time, and you couldn't watch the next movie until you mailed your movie back. It usually took 2 or 3 days for your next movie to arrive. Is it me, or does its kind of seem like Blockbuster had the better deal?

So, how did they manage to fail? Netflix has, and still does have policies that serve their customers. Blockbuster's late fees did nothing but serve the needs of Blockbuster.

I am sure Blockbuster justified the fees by insisting they encouraged customers to bring their movies back sooner. If that was their goal, why didn't they offer discounts on the next movie rental if a customer brought a movie back within 24 hours? What does Zig Ziglar say? "You can have everything in life you want if you help enough people get what they want." We will get in to this more in a later chapter.

As long as you are creating value for other people. and improving lives, you will succeed. That's not to say you won't experience setbacks. If you aren't experiencing challenges in your life, then you are shorting yourself and not living up to your potential.

The Problem with Marketing

John Wanamaker, the founder of Macy's department store is famously quoted as saying "Half the money I spend on advertising is being wasted; the trouble is, I don't know which half." The real trouble with modern marketing is that there are so many ways to spend your time and your money.

There is a steady stream of new social media platforms to reach audiences on. Each platform is churning in a turbulent sea of popularity contests. While some are rising up, others are losing grip on the attention of their users and fading away into obscurity.

I've sat through conferences and read articles that said businesses should be active on all social media platforms. Especially the new ones. As the new platforms grow, any audiences that you have, will expand with the platform as it grows. It is also much cheaper to advertise on a new platform. Meanwhile, it is getting more competitive. Advertising costs are increasing on the large platforms. Everything is getting more expensive. Then, I read about, and hear other speakers at conferences talk about the opposite. Ignore the new social media platforms. Concentrate on the ones that you know well. Only use the social media platforms where your audience is.

All of them do agree that a business will never survive if it relies only on social media advertising. Never. Audiences change too much. Costs are ever-increasing. Competitors will always find a way to do what you do, cheaper, faster, and better. What else can you do then?

Search engine marketing and SEO is just as

treacherous. There is a never-ending deluge of algorithm changes and policy updates. Some can turn web-traffic off overnight and completely wipe out entire industries. I know of SEO businesses that lost their business overnight when Google made some major changes in the algorithm. It changed how websites are ranked and almost completely negated their entire strategy.

What about affiliate marketing? Affiliate marketing is usually a sales-based commission. It is paid out to another company or website for traffic, leads, and sales that they bring to your company.

The downside to affiliate marketing is that you don't own your traffic. Affiliates can shut off the flow of website visitors just as easily as they turn it on. Often times, you are left bidding against your competitors for affiliate links. If you get outbid, you could see a huge percentage of your sales vanish.

It is also very difficult to control your branding

and messaging through affiliates. Each affiliate has their very own identity and messaging. If you force affiliates to use your own messaging and graphics, it can come off looking like an ad, which can backfire on you.

Another problem -- it can be difficult to figure out if an affiliate is helping sales. Or if they are taking credit for a sale that might have already happened without the affiliate.

Affiliates can also compete against you on keywords and search rankings that can drive up your advertising costs.

Don't get me wrong, affiliate marketing has its place in your strategy. When done correctly, it can expose your product to people who have never encountered your brand. Affiliate marketing is an awesome way to fill the top of your sales funnel. It's a terrible way to filter people into the bottom of your sales funnel.

Although email marketing is by far my most favorite channel, it still comes with its own set of limitations. I mostly want to point them out so that more people will be scared of email marketing and I can enjoy less competition. I'm only half-joking. There are several laws regulating email marketing. The U.S. has the CAN-SPAM act that gives rights to people that you are emailing. All of your emails need to have a link that allows people to unsubscribe or opt-out of any future emails from you.

European countries now have GDPR laws that prevent users from abuse of their personal information. You can't sell user information without permission. Double opt-ins are almost mandatory before you can send emails.

There is also a constant battle with your sender reputation. Think of it as a credit score with different email providers. If too many of their users report your emails as spam, don't open them, or don't click on the links in your email, then your sender reputation can suffer. If your score is too low, your emails might end up getting caught by spam traps. The email that you were counting on to bring a lift in your sales never gets viewed by the people you sent it to.

Gmail also uses an algorithm to figure out if your emails are marketing material. When it makes that determination, your emails get sent to the Promotions tab. I don't know if that is a bad thing. It helps manage expectations. I've noticed a decrease in unsubscribes since Gmail has started using the Promotions tab.

My guess is that if your emails are showing up in people's inbox every time you send an email, they will fatigue and unsubscribe. If your emails are going to the Promotions tab, users will expect to see promotional emails there. Fewer people unsubscribe, and fewer people report your emails as spam.

Email has a poor reputation in the marketing industry as being a low performing tool. There are a lot of articles and surveys that suggest Millennials are not using email. This puts into question the future viability of email.

And finally, we have the dinosaur of marketing -- traditional advertising. This is the marketing that has been going on for decades, some of it more than a century. This is your billboards, radio, TV, and mailers. So much of traditional has become so routine to us that we don't even notice it anymore. One of my favorite shows The Shawshank Redemption has a quote in it that goes:

"Andy did like he was told, buffed those shoes to a high mirror shine. The guards simply didn't notice. Neither did I... I mean, seriously, how often do you really look at a man's shoes?"

I can't remember the last time I paid attention to a billboard, opened some junk mail, or listened intently to a radio commercial.

So great! If you are telling me that everything to do with marketing is garbage, what do you recommend that we do?

We are going to get into some marketing principles that will allow your content, advertising, and commercials to rise above the constantly changing, unforgiving landscape of marketing. You will learn what it is that gets attention. How to get the right kind of attention. And what to do with that attention, so that you don't end up like so many other businesses; lost in a proverbial arctic landscape, stranded, fighting off attacks, and no hope of rescue.

The discovery of a lifetime

On a windy, overcast day; one week before Christmas Day in 1994, three friends Christian Hillaire, Eliette Brunel-Deschamps and Jean-Marie Chauvet were exploring caves near the Ardeche River in France, in an area that Jean was very familiar with. He had spent years exploring the area for passages into new cave networks. As dusk settled in around them, they discovered an area with warm air was wisping out of a rubble pile of rocks. They began clawing and tugging at the loose rocks. When they had found the opening, they chiseled it out so that they could squeeze deeper into the cave.

One-by-one they squeezed inside. There, they found themselves perched above a large expanse. None of them had brought any of their speleology equipment. By now dark outside. They decided to return to their vehicles and retrieve their essentials, then return back to the cave. They then used a ladder to drop down into the main chamber 30 feet below.

Awestruck, they pushed through the network of corridors and marveled at the geological formations, ancient animal bones and footprints that were in the cave. It wasn't until they were returning that Christian noticed a red ochre painting on a rock pendant. As they cast their headlamps on the cave walls around them, they began to notice the cave paintings. Christian exuberantly screamed out "They were here!" None of them suspected at the time that what they had discovered was the oldest known cave paintings currently known in existence. The cave paintings depict horses, mammoths, lions, bison, bears, ibex, reindeer, red deer, aurochs, musk-oxen, panthers and owls. Radiocarbon dating estimates that the paintings are between 30,000 - 33,000 years old.

There are so many things that I find fascinating about this. When these cave paintings were made, there were a number of animal species alive that are no longer in existence.

Scientists also found the remains, feces from, and scratches on the cave walls from cave bears. Cave bears were closely related to the brown bear but were about 30% larger. Male cave bears were 800-1100 lbs. As ferocious as they sound, they were vegetarian.

The most interesting part of their discovery; Homo Sapiens had existed 170,000 years before. why were they now starting to paint cave walls? Homo Sapiens had also been co-existing with other branches of the Sapien family. Why weren't Neanderthals painting cave walls? Why did the Homo Sapiens begin to thrive about the same time that they were making cave paintings? Is there a correlation?

We know through skeletal remains that Neanderthals had a shorter frame. Had wider shoulders. A broader chest. Thicker and more dense bones, and musculature than the Homo Sapien.

Other differences were with their brain structures. These differences had an effect on their behaviors and their social interactions. A recent study published in Science Advances, and researchers from the Max Planck Institute for Evolutionary Anthropology found that early Homo sapiens did not have globular brains like we have today.

The study took casts of the brain of early man, by using skulls as a mold. The researchers noted a change that began to occur in the casts between 50,000 and 35,000 years ago. They noticed that the cranial cavities began to globularize, or section off into separate regions. This newly compartmentalized brain allowed for specialization in brain regions. It also allowed simultaneous processes to occur at once, independent of each other.

Brain globularity theories support these findings as the development of the parietal lobes would have helped early Homo sapiens be better at visuospatial abilities and orientation. Additionally, the globulization of the cerebellum would have improved working memory, language and social cognition.

More importantly, Homosapiens had developed the basic tools to create and communicate stories. With the discovery of cave paintings from 30,000 years ago, we have an important clue. We have evidence that early man's brain had developed to the point where he was now expressing himself with elements of story. Story became necessary to address recently developed portions of the brain. Portions that required and craved story to understand the world it was coming in contact with.

What is a story?

The most basic description that you will learn on day one of a creative writing class is that a story has a beginning, middle, and end. A story should also accomplish something and arrive somewhere. There is an often-cited occasion about Ernest Hemingway. He bet a group of his friends that he could write a story that was six words long and would make them cry. He then penned the following story:

For Sale: Baby shoes, never worn.

He won the bet.

A story should also be relatable and needs to contain 2 things:

1. Information.

2. Emotion.

We all tell hundreds of stories everyday with varying mixes of emotion and information. A 13-year-old girl comes home from school, slams the front door, drops her book bag on the floor, sighs and stands motionless, staring at her feet. She just told us a story with not much information in it. After staring inquisitively at her daughter her mom asks, "Is something wrong?"

Without looking up, her daughter points to the door. "I saw a man with a red shirt." Another story. This time without any emotion in it.

Every story has a mix of some information, and some emotion.

What is the purpose of a story?

Why do we tell stories? This is where I venture off into the desolate lands of my own lack of expertise, with only a small grab bag of self-crafted speculation, theories, and limited data set of personal experiences. Now, having said that; I don't think my ideas deviate from current brain science research… too much.

As our early ancestors' brains developed and formed into globules and partition itself; different parts of the brain began to specialize in functions. This evolutionary development allowed us to perform several brain functions simultaneously without interrupting other brain functions. Computer engineers figured out a long time ago that they could get a lot more speed out of a computer if they had multiple processors. Similarly, our brains have multiple processing centers. Each one specializing in unique functions. This also made our brains more efficient, which could have made all of the difference in the world when it came to survival. Even at rest, our brains consume about 20% of our energy. Even a 1% difference in energy consumption by the brain meant 40 fewer calories that needed to be consumed per day. Not much, but that can make all the difference if your species is trying to survive a famine.

There is a show called Trailer Park Boys. One of the characters, Ricky is in jail and is being interviewed. He says "I am smart, and I'm self-smarted. Basically, by myself. Basically, by nature and smoking drugs and stuff, I've self learned myself… People say that books and college is to be for making you smart. But they could also be for to making you get dead… My brain doesn't use enough oxygen because it doesn't have the whole thing filled with different stuff. And if it was full, it's only part full, and that's why I'm alive right now."

Bless poor little Ricky's heart. You know… I feel like his little self-smarted brain is in the right place. I am after all, making basically the same argument. I am not suggesting our early ancestors were less intelligent than the Neanderthal. They might have been for certain aspects. Our brains are actually smaller than Neanderthal's. I am arguing that we had a serious bio-hacked advantage to become more efficient at existing.

As with any advantage, there was also disadvantages. Because the human brain had become siloed, it had to sacrifice some of its interconnectivity, and free-flowing transfer of information.

When you and I are telling a story, our cerebellum is processing speech, gestures, and movements. Our limbic system is producing emotions and basic survival information. Our Frontal cortex is processing information in the story, developing logical analysis, pulling from memories, formulating logical thoughts, and structuring the language. All of this is happening almost completely independently of each other.

As the human brain developed, it became necessary to communicate information to each specialized part of the brain in packets. In other words - stories.

I know we can drill down into brain functions and get extremely technical. As previously stated - I'm no brain scientist, and I want to keep this as simple as possible. Therefore, we are only going to concentrate on 2 parts of the brain:

Frontal Cortex

limbic system

So, what do each of these parts of the brain do? Again, in the interest of simplicity, I am going to make some very generalized and broad categorizations here.

The main function that I want to concentrate on for the frontal cortex is: decision making, cognition, judgement, processing information, and memory. Not all researchers agree exactly what every part of the brain is included in the limbic system. These are the most agreed upon parts of the limbic system: Hippocampus, amygdala, hypothalamus and the thalamus. Each of these play an important and different role in brain function.

Hippocampus - Regulates emotions and is responsible for memories, mostly long-term memories.

Amygdala - We each have two amygdalas-- one on each side of the brain, which are responsible for emotions and memories that relate to our survival instincts. Emotions like fear, and anger. Or memories, like a dog bite.

Hypothalamus - releases neurochemicals that control emotions and behaviors.

Thalamus - Relays sensory information and regulates consciousness, sleep, and alertness.

The limbic system is the reptilian portion of the brain. This is where a bulk of our emotions and our basic survival needs originate.

Continuing on in my sojourn in the barren desert of my lack of expertise. My theory is that logistically, the limbic system and the frontal cortex are about as far from each other as could be possible. Because of their location relative to each other, there are no direct synaptic connections to each other.

Think of your brain as a large corporation. Within that corporation, there will be different departments, all with their own functions and responsibilities.

Every department in a corporation tends to develop their own procedures, policies, culture, and even their own language. On a macro-level we can see the same thing within countries, in regions, between different countries and different continents.

We know that our logical and conscious thinking occurs in the cortex region of the brain. This is also where our language is formed. When information is relayed from the limbic system to the frontal cortex, it arrives through several partitions and a long series of synapses and chemical transfers.

Needless to say, things are going to get a bit messy. Because the limbic system does not have access to the language portion of our brain, thoughts from the limbic system are not going to arrive as words or a neatly packaged idea.

The limbic system has its very own language. The

limbic system has access to a complex array of neurochemicals that control our emotions and the way we feel. The best way we have of understanding what the limbic system wants, or needs is through emotions.

Think back to the last time you were scared. Did you become aware of your fear because a voice in your head said "This is an unsafe scenario. There is 84.725% chance that we are going to become injured unless we take safety precautions. I advise that we run at maximum velocity until we arrive at a safer location."

No, you probably FELT scared.

Thoughts that have to do with survival arrives to our conscious mind, our frontal cortex as a feeling - an emotion. The language of your limbic system is emotion.

Albert Einstein is quoted as saying "Those who understand interest earn it, those who don't, pay it." I would suggest that emotional value is the same. Those that understand emotional value can control it. Those that don't, will be controlled by it. A book that I would recommend is Switch: How to Change when Change is Hard by Chip and Dan Heath.

Although Chip and Dan are not the first people to use the analogy, they are the most well known for their comparison. They compare a person's emotions to an elephant, and logic to the rider on the elephant.

Most of the time, the rider is along for the ride. If the elephant wants to go somewhere, the rider does not have much say in where they go. However, if the rider is persistent and uses a lot of energy and coercion, he can get the elephant to go where he wants. Even if he does change the course of the elephant, he will not be able to maintain control for a very long time.

The rider has learned that it is much easier to justify the actions of the elephant, rather than try to control it.

"Well, you see...:" the rider will explain "We are

extremely thirsty. That's why we are heading to the water right now."

"But I'm different." I can hear you saying to yourself "I don't make emotional decisions. I am 100% rational!" I am sure you are... I am sure you are.

Marketing professor Raj Raghunathan, and Ph.D. student Szu-Chi Huang of the McCombs School of Business conducted a marketing study. In the study, they showed participants two photos of chickens. One image was of a healthy and plump looking chicken. The other photo was of a thin and sickly-looking chicken. The participants were told the plump chicken was a natural chicken. They were then told that the thin chicken was genetically engineered.

Half of the participants were told that natural chickens were healthy. They were also told that the natural chickens did taste good. They were then told that the genetically engineered chickens did taste good. The other half of the group was told the opposite information.

The participants said that they preferred the natural chickens but for different reasons. One group claimed it was because they valued a healthy chicken over the taste. The other group claimed to value taste over what the chicken looked like. Both groups had made emotional decisions about the chickens. In other words, the elephants had wandered off in a direction, and their riders were making justifications.

To illustrate this, use yourself as a study. Think of two products that are similar but with different brand names. Ford or Chevrolet. Charmin or Cottenelle. Mac or PC. Canon or Nikon. Maybelline or Covergirl. Once you have your product, ask yourself why you prefer one over the other. Most of the time, the reasons for picking a favorite brand will not be quantifiable or based on facts. One that I have heard many times is "I use Chevron gasoline in my car because it seems to run better". Another inner dialogue I hear me telling myself is "I've tried other browsers, but Chrome works better". A coworker was recently telling me that he has an unknown aversion to purchasing Texaco gas for his car. When he stopped and thought about it, he realized it was because Texaco uses red and black as their main colors. Red and black would suggest to our elephants that it was dangerous and to be avoided. He preferred Chevron gas because they use a nice calming blue as their dominant color. Blue suggests that it is clean and calm and can be trusted.

I observed something similar while waiting in line at a grocery store. I was behind an individual. He had on gym shorts and a cut-off t-shirt. This was in the beginning of January. So, I made two assumptions. Since it was somewhere around 0 degrees outside, I assumed he was coming from the gym. 2.) He was getting on top of a New Year's resolution to exercise and eat better. Nothing seemed very remarkable to me about him beyond the way he was dressed. Then I noticed what he was placing on the conveyor belt for checkout. Everything he was buying was green; celery, green apples, lettuce, green peppers, cabbage. Lean Cuisine microwave dinners that had green packaging, cereal in a green box.

The entire shopping cart full of green foods, or foods with green packaging. There was no exception. Every single item was green. This was beyond coincidence. He had wandered around the store looking for healthy foods to eat, and to his limbic system, green= healthy. His elephant was certainly doing the shopping that night.

At least his elephant was trying to go make healthy decisions for him. Rarely does mine. If we slip on our lab coat, affix our pocket protector, and look at this man's shopping cart under a microscope. There is nothing that indicates green foods are more healthy than other foods. In his defense, with the exception of a green donut, or mint chocolate ice cream that are too unhealthy for you.

If we remove the lab coat and peer down into our chest cavity and listen to what our emotions have to say. I don't know about you, but when I ponder on how the color green makes me feel. I conjure up images of lush lawns sprinkled with shimmering droplets of dew. Expansive and rolling hills of clover. Lush, billowing trees, springing with fluttering leaves. I think of air that is so clean and crisp it almost snaps when I breath its in. I feel vibrant and recharged. These are the emotional values that are associated with, whether I consciously realize it or not. These are the attributes that are attached to a product when it has a green label.

The problem with relaying emotions

Giving information to someone is a very straightforward and easy process. The dog is brown. The light is on. The bread is gone. Informational statements are straightforward and there isn't a lot of ways that we can misinterpret that information.

Anyone that has been in an emotional relationship will tell you that they can, and often do get murky and complicated. We have a very hard time understanding what our own limbic system wants. It is more difficult to understand what another person's reptile brain is after.

Consider this quote by Marcel Duchamp:

> *"As soon as we start putting our thoughts into words and sentences everything gets distorted, language is just no damn good—I use it because I have to, but I don't put any trust in it. We never understand each other."*

There is however, the flipside to that idea. When there is an emotional understanding, a connection is made, and pure communication occurs.

Chris Voss was a former FBI hostage negotiator and author of the book Never Split the Difference, Negotiating as if Your Life Depended on it. Chris is one of the most well practiced and experienced individuals when it comes to dealing with emotions and emotionally charged situations. Chris has a career dealing with the limbic system's amygdala. Chris says, "Emotions aren't the obstacles to a successful negotiation, They are the means."

A story is a vehicle for one person to pass both

information and emotion to another person.

Do you ever have a moment when you say something in jest, but then when you think about it, there's actually a lot of truth behind what you said?

One time I was talking to a friend. He asked, "Why does my mom always exaggerate every detail of her stories?"

I said "Because, to her, when telling a story, it is more important to maintain emotional integrity than it is to maintain truthfulness about the informational details in a story. If she is telling you about how scared she was, she is going to exaggerate the scary details of the story in order to deliver the magnitude of the fear she was experiencing." I was kidding when I had originally said that, but I really do think that to her, she is maintaining the integrity of her stories because her limbic system is in fact, telling the truth.

The Equation

Something that often intrigues me, is why do I buy things that are gimmicky or inferior even when I know they are? Packaging fascinates me. The use of colors, geometry, typography, textures, forms and static or fluid shapes. I love a product with a well thought out design. I still buy some products despite poor design because it was cheaper. On the other hand, I would pay 2,3 or 4 times as much for a product because it was packaged better. What's up with that? We all make some illogical purchases.

Pizza for example. I don't like Little Ceaser's pizza. I have yet to eat their pizza and twenty minutes later, with any sort of honesty, say to myself "Well, I'm glad I ate that." Yet, every week I find myself sitting at their drive thru, ordering their pizza. I could get a pizza that I liked much better for 2 or 3 dollars more a few blocks away. Then why don't I?

For years I wondered about not only my own behavior but other purchasers too. Then one day I listened to a Ted Talk by Simon Sinek. "How Great Leaders Inspire Action" It is a popular talk, that has made such an impact on people, that I hear it referenced constantly.

Understandably, it had a large influence on me and shaped much of the way that I viewed this behavior in my own life.

Simon Talks about what he calls the Golden Circle. A target like circle with three rings. How, what and Why. The inner circle being "Why". The "Why" portion of our brain resides in our cerebral cortex at the base of our brain. If you can answer to, and speak to that portion of a person's mind, you can affect their decision making. I love what he has to say in his talk. It was the first time I had ever heard anyone explain why something like an Apple computer was so much more popular than a Dell computer. It all had to do with the way Steve Jobs thought of his product. Simon Sinek Explains: I use Apple because they're easy to understand and everybody gets it. If Apple were like everyone else, a marketing message from them might sound like this. "We make great computers. They're beautifully designed, simple to use and user friendly. Want to buy one?" Neh. And that's how most of us communicate. That's how most marketing is done. That's how most sales are done. And that's how most of us communicate interpersonally. We say what we do. we say how we're different or how we're better and we expect some sort of a behavior, a purchase, a vote, something like that. Here's our new law firm. We have the best lawyers with the biggest clients. We always perform for our clients who do business with us. Here's our new car. It gets great gas mileage. It has leather seats. Buy our car. But it's uninspiring. Here's how Apple actually communicates." Everything we do, we believe in challenging the status quo. We believe in thinking differently. The way we challenge the status quo is by making our products beautifully designed, simple to use and user friendly. We just happen to make great computers. Want to buy one?" Totally different right? You're ready to buy a computer from me. All I did was reverse the order of information.

I still had lingering questions that I couldn't understand. Why was I buying crappy pizza when I couldn't really see how they were answering to my "why"? I didn't see the answer as a binary, on or off, yes/no question. It was muddled in between. I wanted an equation. A formula. A plug and play device to understand what was happening here.

It seemed to me that I couldn't redraw the picture until I turned it upside down. I knew "Why". But I didn't know why "Why". I know that whenever I ask someone "Why", the answer I am always given is a story. And a story always answered my question. So that was my answer to why "Why". It's a story problem.

Storytelling is how we pass two types of information. The physical attributes of the story. These are the parts that deal with Who, What, Why, When, Where and How. This is the part of the story where your frontal cortex is absorbing information and developing an understanding based on the facts.

The second part of storytelling that is passed is the emotional attributes. The way it makes you feel. The portion of the story that makes you mad. The part that makes you smile, cry, laugh, ashamed, playful or sad.

Because the emotional attributes felt so ethereal, individualistic, and mystical, I found it the most undervalued and underutilized in marketing. Yet it is the most crucial part. I still couldn't understand why.

One day at work, I was having a terrible time trying to concentrate on my work. I could feel my mind churning away at something complex. Have you ever been working on your computer and everything was unnecessarily slow? Nothing opened as fast as it usually did. Saving a file took several times longer than it usually does. After investigating, you find a memory intensive program running in the background. That's how I felt that day. The following morning, I woke up and it felt like my brain dropped this equation into my conscious mind. Looking back on it, it seems quite rudimentary. Now find that if I use this equation, it is way easier to wrap my head around how the element of story works. This is the equation:

$V = Ev^n + Pv^n$

V = Value

Ev = Emotional Value

Pv = Physical Value

n = Needs

Another way to think about Value is how desirable something is.

The Emotional Value is how desirable the limbic system of your brain feels like something is.

The Physical Value is how much the frontal cortex of your brain thinks the object or service is worth.

Needs are based on a sliding scale. They are the X-factor. Depending on the need, they can put the elephant in charge of the brain's decisions, or they can put the rider in charge. Needs are based off of Maslow's Hierarchy of Needs, which isn't perfect. It is widely known and the model fits nicely with the story equation.

Maslow explained the needs by arranging them into a pyramid shape. Starting from the bottom and the most important; the needs are physiological needs, Safety needs, Love/belonging, esteem, and then self-actualization is at the top.

Physiological needs

Physiological needs are the physical requirements for human survival. If these requirements are not met, the human body cannot function properly and will fail. Physiological needs are thought to be the most important; they should be met first. This is the first and basic need on the hierarchy of needs. Without them, the other needs cannot follow up. Physiological needs include:

Breathing

Water

Food

Sleep

Clothing

Shelter

Sex

Safety needs

When your physiological needs are relatively satisfied, safety needs then take a precedence and will begin to dominate your behavior. Safety and security needs are about keeping us safe from harm. These include shelter, job security, health, and safe environments. If you do not feel safe in an environment, you will seek to find safety before you attempt to meet any higher level of survival. War, natural disaster, family violence, childhood abuse, are all examples that can threaten your needs for safety.

Safety and Security needs include:

Personal security

Emotional security

Financial security

Health and wellbeing

Safety needs against accidents/illness and their adverse impacts

Social belonging

After physiological and safety needs are met, the third level of human needs is desire to feel involved and a sense of belonging. Lack of social belonging due to neglect, shunning, and ostracism, can have negative effects on a person's ability to form and maintain emotionally relationships in general. According to Maslow, humans need to feel a sense of belonging and acceptance among social groups, regardless whether these groups are large or small. For example, some large social groups may include clubs, co-workers, religious groups, professional organizations, sports teams, gangs, and online communities. Some examples of small social connections include family members, intimate partners, mentors, colleagues, and confidants. Many people become susceptible to loneliness, social anxiety, and clinical depression in the absence of this love or belonging element. This need for belonging may overcome the physiological and security needs, depending on the strength of the peer pressure

Social Belonging needs include:

Friendships

Intimacy

Family

Esteem

Esteem needs deal with recognition, status, importance, and respect from others. All humans have a need to feel respected. This includes the need to have self-esteem and self-respect. Esteem presents the typical human desire to be accepted and valued by others. People often engage in a profession or hobby to gain recognition. These activities give the person a sense of contribution or value. Low self-esteem or an inferiority complex may result from imbalances during this level in the hierarchy. People with low self-esteem often need respect from others; they may feel the need to seek fame or glory. However, fame or glory will not help the person to build their self-esteem until they accept who they are internally. Psychological imbalances such as depression can hinder the person from obtaining a higher level of self-esteem or self-respect.

Most people have a need for stable self-respect and self-esteem. Maslow noted two versions of esteem needs: a "lower" version and a "higher" version. The "lower" version of esteem is the need for respect from others. This may include a need for status, recognition, fame, prestige, and attention. The "higher" version manifests itself as the need for self-respect. For example, the person may have a need for strength, competence, mastery, self-confidence, independence, and freedom. This "higher" version takes guidelines, the "hierarchies are interrelated rather than sharply separated". This means that esteem and the subsequent levels are not strictly separated; instead, the levels are closely related.

Self-actualization

Maslow describes this level as the desire to accomplish everything that one can, to become the most that one can be. Some people may perceive or focus on this need very specifically. For example, someone might have a strong desire to become an ideal parent. For others, it may be expressed in paintings, pictures, or inventions. Maslow believed that to understand this level of need, the person must not only achieve the previous needs, but master them. Self-Actualization - A person's motivation to reach his or her full potential. As shown in Maslow's Hierarchy of Needs, a person's basic needs must be met before self-actualization can be achieved.

Self-transcendence

In his later years, Maslow explored further dimension of needs, while criticizing his own vision on self-actualization. By this later theory, the self only finds its actualization in giving itself to some higher outside goal, in altruism and spirituality. He equated this with the desire to reach the infinite. "Transcendence refers to the very highest and most inclusive or holistic levels of human consciousness, behaving and relating, as ends rather than means, to oneself, to significant others, to human beings in general, to other species, to nature, and to the cosmos."

For the last 30,000 years, mankind has been hardwired to pay attention to stories. Ever since our early ancestors' brains began to compartmentalize, stories became the emotional vehicle for our limbic systems to relay information from one person to another.

Unfortunately, we don't have any physical evidence of it, but I am certain that before early man was painting on cave walls, he was telling stories to other people. We have relics of ancient fables, and legends that were passed on from one generation to the next. But the problem with oral history and legends is that they are not permanently recorded.

The oldest story we have of a written story is the story of Gilgamesh. It was recorded on clay tablets about 4000 years ago. But oral narratives existed for 10's of thousands of years before written language had enough time to catch up with spoken words.

The magic of storytelling is what research reveals to us about storytelling, you can plant ideas, concepts, and emotions into someone else's brain.

No, I'm serious. Researchers measured brainwaves and activity in certain parts of people's brains. They found that when someone told them a story, the brainwaves of the listeners began to sync up with the brainwaves of the storyteller. By telling a story, the listener's and storyteller's brainwaves synced, and it activated similar parts of the brain between the storyteller and the listener.

Other research has shown that elements of a story are 22 times more easily recalled than just facts alone.

When telling a story, clearly the emotional value is the enigma. Misunderstood and so it has been avoided because it can't easily be quantified. If we look at the equation for story $S = Ev^n + Pv^n$. Think of this as the Yin and Yang. In a healthy system there is equal physical and emotional balance.

Most of our emotional needs originate somewhere in the limbic system. Because of this it is difficult to realize an emotional need. If I am thirsty, my mouth gets dry and I know I need a drink. An easy to identify indicator. If I have an emotional need to feel accepted, I might just have a general feeling of anxiety, but I probably don't know why I am feeling this way.

The reason emotional and physical value is multiplied by (n) need is because we all have varying degrees of needs.

In an extreme example let's suppose you were drowning. You would have a high-level need for oxygen. Your story would have nothing to do with emotions. You could care less that you have an emotional need to feel trusted. You are about 10 seconds away from death if you don't get more oxygen.

As a side tangent, how many times do we do things that are detrimental to our health because of emotional stress? Eat too much because we are sad, disappointed, distracted by a persistent worry. Decompress and shut out problems in front of the TV for an entire afternoon, day or weekend? Work too much. Exercise too much. Shop too much.

Spend too much. Sleep too much. Worry too much.

when iPods were new, Apple released a version of the iPod that had a color display, could play movies and had a 30 or 80gb hard drive. To compete, Microsoft created a 30 and 80gb MP3 player. Microsoft called them the Zune. The Zunes could also play movies, could easily accept any music that you wanted to put on it. The iPods would not accept music unless it was imported awkwardly through iTunes. The Zunes also had games that could be put on them. Their screens were also larger.

In most aspects, the Zune could outperform and had better features than the iPod. It was a better product on the physical value of the equation. Can I go to the store and buy a Zune today? No. They were discontinued in 2011. So, what went wrong? Did Microsoft not have enough money to put into advertising? I doubt it. Were people not aware that the Zune was a better product? Nope. I've seen parody videos poking fun of how much information Microsoft tries to put on packaging. I could go on for chapters about what Apple has done right. They are an excellent case study on this topic. For the sake of not being redundant, I will conclude with this idea: At the time of this writing, Apple currently owns 10% of the currency in the U.S. through cash on hand and assets. For every $10 in your wallet, Apple has $1. Are they successful? Is emotional value powerful? Yes. It is how empires are created and wars are won. Recently I have watched several agencies tap into the emotional value of client's product and instantly realize huge market gains.

For the past 10 years, Dove Beauty Products has been quietly redefining and enlarging the world's idea of what beauty is. I was like most people. Oblivious to their mission. Then they created a video that showed several women sitting down answering several questions from an FBI sketch artist who was behind a curtain. He could not see the women. The women were simply prompted with questions to help them describe their own faces. We are all our own worst critic and they all over exaggerated the flaws and imperfections. The sketch artist sketched the hideous details the women described about themselves. The women were excused. Individuals that had recently met each of the women sat down in front of the sketch artist. They described the women's faces that they had just met -- who had just described themselves to the sketch artist. When they were done, there were two drawings of each woman. One as the women saw themselves and another as someone else sees them. Both drawings were hung next to each other and then the women were allowed to look at both drawings.

The differences were stark and shocking. The women were surprised and humbled at the differences. The video had a powerful emotional message. Not once did it show a bar of soap, or a bottle of shampoo. They never discussed a new cleansing technology. It never mentioned moisturizers or conditioners. Almost no physical property of any Dove product was ever mentioned. On paper, this concept makes almost no sense to an analytical.

How does an ad that does not mention a product's benefits out-perform an ad that might scientifically demonstrate the plentitude of astonishing features of a product? The power of Emotional Value.

What sort of gains did Dove see from the video? They finished the year off with a 3% growth and an extra $1.5 billion in revenue. But that was just short-term growth. The goal with the campaign was long term growth, and brand health.

I'm not sure if it is conscious or not, since viewing the video, I have noticed my wife has slowly been replacing the products in the bathroom with Dove products. Do I think Dove products work as well as their competitor's? In other words, do I think Dove's Physical Value is as good as the other leading brands? If I did a blind test, I don't think I would pick them every time. Is emotional value powerful? Very much.

A few years ago, Coca-Cola had some ads that had me slamming my hand on a table and excitedly proclaiming "They get it! They know what they are doing and it's working!" The first ad showed Coke machines being set up in one part of the world with a camera and a screen in front of the Coke machine with a camera and large tv monitor. A corresponding camera and tv monitor was set up in another location in another part of the world. The commercial showed several people sharing a Coke with someone in another country and continent. For decades Coke has positioned itself as a global product. but the subtext that was more powerful, the emotional value was that Coke brings people of all backgrounds together as a human family. all over the world and people in one country sharing a Coke with someone in a different country.

Coke also pulled advertising after typhoon

Yolanda hit the Philippines. They took the money that they would have spent on the advertising and donated it for relief funds for those affected by the typhoon. The positive emotion, buzz and PR generated by this strategy created more attention than any advertising they could have done. Coca-Cola completely understands the value of their story, and how to leverage their emotional value. It has paid off immensely short term and long term.

This is not the first time Coca-Cola has carefully crafted themselves into a position that is synonymous with a positive emotion. Did you know that the iconic image that we all imagine when we think of Santa Claus was developed in a large part by Coca-Cola? Coca-Cola has been using advertising with Santa Claus since the 1920's. Before that time, the depictions of Santa were all over the place and varied quite a bit. Coca-Cola began depicting the image of Santa as we know him now - an older man, white beard, red suit, jolly, and a big, round belly. It has taken Coca-Cola decades to accomplish this, but they have nestled themselves right up there in our minds with one of the most happy, cheerful holidays that we celebrate.

Something that I could never understand was; why an actor or an athlete was paid more in one day than most of us would see after a year of working 40-hour work weeks. Why did pretending to be someone you are not, or throwing a ball through a hoop, or whacking a ball into a hole, or throwing, or kicking a ball to another person create so much value that it justified this type of salary?

When you look at the physical value, it makes almost no sense. When you pair up the physical value with the emotional value it starts to come into focus. It starts to demonstrate the power of the emotional value.

Their customers are their fans and audience members. Imagine the reaction of a spectator who just saw their team win in the final seconds of a game. Now think of someone who just discovered their favorite brand of soda was on sale. Different reactions, right? I have to admit, I would enjoy watching someone jumping up and down and screaming in delight and running up and down the snack aisle of the grocery store hugging strangers after they discovered they saved $1.20 on a 12 pack of Coke. Or what if a high school team won the state championship and the fans smirked to themselves, shook their heads affirmatively while looking around to make sure no one saw their jubilation, and then quietly shuffled back to their homes. There is a huge difference in emotional involvement in each situation.

What are some emotional values? Here is a list of a few of the emotional values that are available for you to use:

accepted

accepting

accomplished

acknowledged

admired

alive

amused

appreciated

appreciative

approved of

attention

capable

challenged

clear (not confused)

competent

confident

developed

educated

empowered

focused

forgiven

forgiving

free

fulfilled

grown or growing

happy

heard

helped

helpful

important

in control

included

independent

interested

knowledgeable

listened to

loved

needed

noticed

open

optimistic

privacy

productive

protected

proud

reassured

recognized

relaxed

respected

safe

satisfied

secure

significant

successful

supported

treated fairly

understanding

understood

useful

valued

worthy

Let's run a simple test. Imagine you own a company. You make shoes. The number one feature about your shoes is their weight. They are the lightest shoe ever made. You tell people "My shoes are the lightest shoes ever made. Buy them.". A few do, but for the most part, you are ignored.

"They are the lightest shoes ever made. Why isn't everyone buying my shoes?" you wonder to yourself. Without adding any emotional value to your product - I hate to tell you, but your lightest shoes ever made are going to languish and fail in the market. I absolutely guarantee it.

What are you to do to become the thriving, successful entrepreneur? I'm glad you asked. Let's grab an emotional value at random of the list. Free. You decide that the emotional value you want use is "free". You tell your next potential customer. "Experience true freedom when you run in these shoes." Your customer doesn't pull out his wallet, but he pauses. You have his attention. He's curious. He wouldn't consider your shoes if you had told him that these shoes are light, because that emotional value is ambiguous. It's not clear how light shoes can help him in his life. But freedom? You are starting to talk to his inner-elephant. He realizes that you might have a solution to a problem. Your shoes could make his life easier.

At this moment, it isn't clear how you address that problem, so he is willing to invest a few seconds to find out more. You continue "These are the lightest shoes in the world." You've added the physical value into the equation. Suddenly you have a viable and valuable product on the market.

The stronger you can assert your claim that your shoes bring freedom, the more successful your shoes will be. "Experience true freedom. Because these are the lightest shoes in the world, you can run further, run faster, run longer, and feel better running."

There are two traps that businesses fall into:

The number one trap that most businesses fall into is that they think they are selling a product or service. Successful businesses are in the market of making stories.

The second trap is closely related. You are in the business of helping your customers find their story. NOT YOUR OWN.

I started this book 7 years ago. It seemed like, as

soon as I came up with the idea to write this book, everyone was suddenly talking about storytelling in business. I eventually dropped the idea - but, to be honest, I was sick of hearing about story. But very few people were talking about it in the right way. I kept seeing people use story to tell their OWN story. If there is one thing I want you to remember from this book is that people don't give a damn about your story. Our inner-elephants, our reptile brains are extremely narcissistic. They only care about your story to the extent that it pertains to them. "How does this story relate to me?" That's all your reptile brain wants to know.

SAAS (Service as a software) companies are the worst at this. This is from a landing page of a highly ranked SAAS company:

"Our benchmarked employee survey, intuitive culture software and seasoned culture strategy team gives you unparalleled insight into what's happening within your organization, plus guidance on exactly where to focus next."

Um...what just happened? I read that sentence and my brain dropped into a coma. First of all, starting their positioning statement with "Our"? That's a personal foul. 15-yard penalty. 2nd down. "Benchmarked employee survey"? Look - nobody knows what that is. I am sure the person that wrote that doesn't even know what that is. Maybe that's a thing. I'm not in the employee survey business, so maybe that's something that is real. I'll overlook it. Moving on.

"Intuitive culture software"? Really? Out of all the words out there to choose from, and "Intuitive culture software" is what you came up with?

You see, that's why I decided to pick this book back up and finish it. This was the first result on a Google search. There is terrible copy everywhere. Here is the deal - your limbic system is busy. It has an important job. It has to keep you alive. It cannot afford to spend much time on anything. If you don't deliver something that is threatening, novel or pleasurable within the first 3-5 seconds of someone interacting with your brand, they are off scanning something else for something that is threatening, novel, or pleasurable.

That is why you should front-load your copy, videos, and graphics with something that is one of those three things: Threatening, novel, or pleasurable.

Let's try rewriting that statement.

"Learn what beliefs and passions are driving your business so that you can use the best parts of your company culture to drive success."

Learning From Hollywood

There is a lot we as marketers can learn from Hollywood. I find it curious that as marketers, we have to pay to put an ad in front of an audience member. That same person will pay to go see a movie. Nobody wants to see an ad, everyone wants to see a movie. This goes back to the old adage that - No one likes to be sold to, but everyone likes to buy.

We are pre-wired to pay attention to stories. We enjoy stories.

The challenge with selling and telling a story is that it is a bit like a performing a magic trick. You have to be subtle, quick handed, or have a good distraction. If your audience catches you playing to their emotions, you become cheesy or creepy. This is the art of storytelling.

Lucky for us, there have several intelligent people that have demystified this technique for us.

In filmmaking and screenwriting, each movie has to give the audience an emotional value. The better the film does in delivering that, the more people that like it. In movies, the screenwriter has to sell you on the emotional value without you noticing. There is a technique that deepens your empathy towards the main character, giving you a reason to care when they are faced with challenges or facing a foe.

A talented screenwriter, Blake Snyder wrote a book about this called "Save the cat". He breaks the techniques to screenwriting down into easy to understand concepts. The first concept he covers is, as the book name implies is called Save the Cat. An easy and common sleight of hand to deliver the emotional value. In a movie, the main character will do something, like save a cat, help a neighbor with their groceries, or be kind to a stranger. The technique instantly builds empathy for the main character. Watch for it in the next movie you watch. It is used everywhere.

How can brands use empathy marketing?

I know I said that it is not about your brand's story. Like movies, you have to persuade your audience that they should care about your product(s) and your brand. Most of the time, we should do that with product benefits, but as a branding tool, it is possible to do both.

Another Super Bowl ad that I loved was a series made for Johnsonville, about their bratwursts. They worked with the ad agency Droga 5. The commercials were written by Johnsonville employees. Some of them are a bit odd, but that adds to the genuine feel of the videos. My favorite is an ad called The Chase. Here is the dialogue from it:

Johnsonville Sausage employee Brett pitches his

idea for a company commercial. The scene opens with a car chase where semi-trucks, bikers and grandmas on scooters are pursuing a giant Johnsonville grill on wheels. When the driver discovers that his co-pilot left the brats on the grill again, they decide to pull over and put them to good use. The commercial ends with everyone together, feasting on the brats ... and with an explosion for good measure.

Another ad is called Jeff and His Forest Friends. It starts with a text graphic that says, "At Johnsonville, our people are responsible for everything". Even the commercials." Then Jeff is shown, and his ad is portrayed while he describes it.

He says "Hi, I'm Jeff. In my Johnsonville commercial, we open in the forest. I'm out in the wild eating my breakfast and all of a sudden, a raccoon come up and asked me

'What are you eating?'

Told him 'Johnsonville breakfast sausage, fully

cooked and ready to eat.'

Squirrel comes up and asks, 'Tell me some more about that?'

So, I told the squirrel 'Tastes great. It's got great texture.'

Turkey comes up and asked if that comes in any other flavors, and I say 'Yep! Comes in original'

Porcupine comes up and he says, 'Does that come in patties?'

I said 'Yep! They're new!'

Wolf comes in and says 'Howd'ya learn to talk to animals?'

And I said 'Books!'

And wolf says 'Touché' and we had a good laugh about that.

That's a breakfast sausage commercial made the Johnsonville way"

I like these because the ads highlight benefits and features of Johnsonville products. They involve great elements of some literal storytelling. It builds brand empathy because we begin to know, like and trust a brand. They entrust their employees enough to let them create their own commercials.

A screenwriter's favorite trick in a movie is to show the main character being nice to an animal. The main character usually does this within the first few minutes of the movie. It might seem like something minor, but that is all it takes for us, the audience, to esteem the character as someone that is like-able. It is a very subtle technique, but as mentioned before, once it has been pointed out to you, you will notice it everywhere.

Don't make the mistake of thinking that this strategy only works in Hollywood. It also works in marketing. There are a number of brands that are doing a great job at this. Subaru recently produced a series of videos showing dogs learning to drive cars, with older dogs trying to teach them how to drive. There is a carwash video that portrays dogs trying to wash a muddy Subaru.

Subaru created a website landing page called "Subaru loves pets". It is part of a larger campaign called "The Subaru Love Promise". They state, "Love means being more than a car company". The Subaru Love Promise is our vision to show love and respect to all people at every interaction with Subaru. Together with our retailers, we are dedicated to making the world a better place.

Customer's Journey

A constant battle that marketers face is knowing what interaction, or series of interactions, what benefit, what feature, what blog post, what ad, what email, what landing page, what promotion persuaded a customer to make a purchase decision. What makes it even more difficult to understand this is that when you ask a customer, they don't even know. Remember the analogy of the elephant and the rider? When you ask a customer why they bought, you are asking the rider why he steered the elephant to a destination. Most of the time, the rider was along for the ride. He doesn't have a clue why the elephant went that direction.

We don't have a clue why our limbic system made the call to purchase something. We have some feelings and emotions about it, but those are up to interpretation, are subjective, and change with the context of our memories.

As marketers, we gather as much data about people as we can, but it is still a guess about what the most influential interaction was. We want to understand our attribution. Who or what gets credit for the sale?

If I asked you what your favorite movie was, and then asked you what one scene makes that whole movie your favorite. Would you be able to give me answer?

We all have our favorite scene in our favorite movie, but usually there are supporting scenes that build up to that one scene. There are also other scenes that we enjoy as much. It's rare that we can give 100% credit to one movie scene for making a movie our absolute favorite movie. In other words, if we cut everything out of the entire movie and you had watched that 2- or 3-minute segment of the show without the context of the rest of the story, would you still consider that your favorite movie? Maybe not.

Unless your product has no differentiators and it is the cheapest product, or if your product is a necessity item with no other competition, then your customers have journey to travel through during the consideration phase of purchasing. I don't care if your product is fifty cent pack of gum, or a twenty-million-dollar luxury yacht, there is still a consideration phase for your product. There is still a customer journey for your product. Bearing in mind that:

People like to buy, but hate to be sold to

People will pay to be entertained, but have to be incentivized to see an ad

Marketers have a story problem. How do you tell a story while persuading people to want your product or service?

The Hero's Journey

There is a long string of psychiatrists, professors, and writers who have been building upon the idea of the monomyth or universal story. Joseph Campbell first popularized the idea of the hero's journey when he wrote the book "The Hero With a Thousand Faces", which expanded upon the theories that were developed by the famous psychiatrist Carl Jung. Jung had written about a monomyth, or template that all legends and myths fit into.

They explored the concept that there are elemental steps that a character goes through in a story. All though each step is not required for a story - you can observe the pattern in most movies that you watch and most novels that you read.

In 2007 Christopher Vogler, a writer for Disney wrote a seven-page memo called "A practical guide to The Hero With a Thousand Faces".

I like Christopher's stages of a journey the most. His steps are:

The Ordinary World: the hero is seen in his/her everyday life

The Call to Adventure: the inciting incident of the story

Refusal of the Call: the hero experiences some hesitation to answer the call

Meeting with the Mentor: the hero gains the supplies, knowledge, and confidence needed to commence the adventure

Crossing the First Threshold: the hero commits wholeheartedly to the adventure

Tests, Allies and Enemies: the hero explores the special world, faces trial, and makes friends and enemies

Approach to the Innermost Cave: the hero nears the center of the story and the special world

The Ordeal: the hero faces the greatest challenge yet and experiences death and rebirth

Reward: the hero experiences the consequences of surviving death

The Road Back: the hero returns to the ordinary world or continues to an ultimate destination

The Resurrection: the hero experiences a final moment of death and rebirth so he (or she) is pure when he reenters the ordinary world

Return with the Elixir: the hero returns with something to improve the ordinary world

These stages are broken down into 3 steps of the journey:

Departure

Initiation

Return

From the marketer's perspective, we talk about the customer's journey as steps in the sales funnel.

Awareness - Someone first encounters the product

or difficulty in their life.

Interest - Something sparks an interest. There might be something that is appealing about the product or realize that there is a solution that exists to their problem.

Consideration - They are either actively or passively considering solutions to their problems.

Intent - They have decided that they are going to do something about their problem or make a purchase.

Evaluation - They are selecting which product to buy and weighing the options.

Purchase - They have selected their best option and made their purchase.

Those steps are usually simplified into 3 areas of the sales funnel:

Top funnel

Mid-funnel

Bottom funnel

You already know where I am going with this, because you can see the overlaps. The easiest way to explain how to turn your marketing script into a captivating and engaging process, that allows a customer to make a purchase decision, rather than you selling to them, is to use terms that marketers are familiar with. Let's break the marketing story process into 6 stages by blending the hero's journey and the customer journey:

Normal life

Agitation

Meet the mentor

The call-to-Action

The rebirth

The return with elixir

Normal Life

This is the status quo. This is where we expect life to be all of the time. No rocking boats. No clouds in the sky. Beautiful, sunny days every day. However, life never seems to stay here for very long. To us, it seems like everyone else has lives that stay here in perpetuity.

In the movie Groundhog Day, Phil is a self-centered news anchor who seems only capable of thinking about himself. Everything is normal until he wakes up and the day and everything is exactly like it was before. And that is the exact problem. Everything is exactly the same. This is the point that Phil departs his normal life.

When Happy Gilmore begins, Happy is trying to make it on a hockey team. Although, his life is anything but normal, that is the status-quo for Happy. In the opening credits, Happy explains that his dad was a huge hockey fan. He loved hockey so much that he ignored his wife. Because she took the backseat to hockey, she divorced her husband and moved to Egypt because there wasn't a hockey rink for hundreds of miles in Egypt. One day at a hockey game, Happy's father got hit with a hockey puck and was killed. Happy was sent to go live with his grandma. As a side note - remember when we were talking earlier about deepening empathy for a character? Ding, ding, ding! Having a main character care for a grandma… that is a definite example of the use of this.

One day, happy doesn't make the cut for the hockey team he was trying out. When he comes home, his girlfriend is leaving him because he is a miserable failure at life. When he goes to his grandma's, her house is being sold along with everything in it because she had not been paying her taxes for the past 10 years. This is when Happy has to leave his normal life. To save his grandma's house, he has to find a way to stop his cycle of failures.

In marketing terms, this stage is someone's life before they are aware of your product. Or the problems they can solve with your product. These are the "Before" picture of a before-and-after photo.

These are the exaggerated video clips in infomercials with someone struggling with routine activities.

Narrator: Do you struggle with drinking from a cup?

A woman is seen taking a drink from a cup, but she tilts the cup back too far causing juice to run down both sides of her face and spill on her shirt. She flinches in shock as the cold liquid soaks her. She jerks the cup away from her face. She spills the rest of the juice all over the place. Freeze frame as the juice is flying towards her in the air. Fade to black and white. A giant red X graphic appears, covering the whole screen.

These people are not anywhere in your sales funnel yet. They are bebopping through life, completely oblivious to you or your product.

I wanted to share a story that my grandpa wrote. Dad was a good-natured, gregarious fellow; who directed his attention and energies toward the outside world and left the raising of the family to Mother. Generally, But not always. Every now and so often he would get the idea one of his knot-headed sons needed a lesson in something or other and then he could be really tough. That happened, when I. was about twelve years old. Twelve years is a bad age for any boy. That's the age when he is too big to be a baby and too young to be a man. About all he can do is run errands and get into trouble.

It all started, when a letter came to our place addressed to a sheep-herder named Jos. We lived on a ranch, one of many in that a real where most everyone owned. a 160-acre plot and the nearest neighbors were barely within earshot of a. 30 -30 rifle. Dad showed me the letter and announced, "Bright and early in the morning you can take that letter to Joe." It howled to high Heaven that I know nothing of Joe's whereabouts, or how to deliver letters and went on to enumerate a dozen or more reasons of why I couldn't do the job during which time had leaned back in the chair and took a short nap. I tried to tip-toe away without waking him but as I rounded the corner he called "First thing in the morning!"

First thing in the morning, long before daylight, "'I was, bounced out of bed and plunked down to the breakfast table where I glared back at a sad-eyed egg and a stack of hotcakes. Mother was busy at the stove. Dad sat opposite me drinking his coffee. He had a habit of inhaling his coffee with a loud 'Whoosh' and then swallowing with a crackling sound. I waited for Mother to turn, around and say

'But Vic, he's only a boy …. but she didn't. Apparently, that issue was already decided. Dad set his cup down and suggested "You better eat." I tried to get a few mouthfuls from plate to mouth through the torrent or tears".

Dad watched impassively 'til my sobs subsided, then leaned closer and said "Now, if you'll listen, I'll tell you how to find Joe." I nodded, and he went onto describe the area where the herd was supposed to be. I heard the first few words and then his voice became a senseless rumble. He. knew I wasn't listening, but he let it go at that. With him, there was always other day coming. Mounted and with a sack. lunch in the, saddle bag, I headed out north-east over Stos's hill and down to the river crossing', then up the river trail to the fork where I climbed out of the river bed and went straight east. That much of my instructions, I remembered. Beyond that, I was but faintly familiar with the country, but I figured I know it well enough to find a whole herd or sheep hidden there-in. But when my instructions ran out so did my progress. My mileage dropped to zero.

The object of my search was somewhere among the thousand-and-one low foothills crouched at the base of the Uinta mountains. It was late spring, and the sheep were 'following- the feed' up from the low country and toward their high summer range. I undertook to penetrate that jungle of hills, and ravines, rocks and brush, pinion and ponderosa, and found myself completely stymied. My horse didn't help any. He knew more than I and he insisted on following the ridges rather than cut crosswise, and between the two of us, I had a hard time just keeping my directions straight. The brush tore my shirt and frayed my patience I got madder and madder. At noon I removed the bridle bit and let my horse graze while I ate lunch and stole a short nap, then on to more of the same. When the sun got dangerously low in the west I headed for home to break the news that there was no such thing as a herd of sheep is that part of the country.

It was dark when I rode in and unsaddled. Dad moseyed out to meet me and I. broke the glad-tidings that no such herd existed. He said "Um-Hum" and strode back to the house.

Next morning, same time, I got bounced out of bed and plunked down at the breakfast table. Same egg, Same hot cakes. Same awful wait while Dad finished his coffee. The only thing different was that I screamed louder and sobbed harder -- all in vain. Daylight found me riding out across Stot's hill and down to the river. The second day was so much like the first there's no use talking about it. Dad met me at the saddle shed that night mid asked "Any luck?" I said "No" and he said 'Well, "I'll be damned!"

Next morning, I ricocheted when I hit the floor and screamed so loud the dogs outside came barking to the door thinking someone, was being butchered. That morning Dad drank a second cup of coffee and had a short nap while he listened me out. I labored the point something awful before I finally wound down. When I worked down to the sulks, and short sniffles, Dad suggested. "You better eat." Another impressive silence, then he hitched his chair, a bit closer and began "Listen, Son." (He always called me Son when he meant, business) "You're going to be riding for that herd, next Christmas unless you settle down to business." He let that sink in. I was flabbergasted. This was more, serious than I thought. After a long pause he went on; "That herd. of sheep is not lost, It's you that's lost, and you're not going to find it 'til you get on the right track. And you won't get on the right track 'til you open up your ears and, listen to what I've been trying to tell you."

I nodded. my sobbing approval and he went on; "Now, for the third time I'm going to tell you how to rind that herd. When you turn east off the river trail, you ride to the top of the first ridge. From there, if you look up toward the foot of the mountain, you will, see a high knob that stands out above the other hills. You ride right to the top of that knob. The going will be easier if you angle off to the left. When you get there, get off your horse and sit down. Spend an hour -- two hours --- spend all the time you want studying the landscape. From there you can see for miles in all directions, when you get it mapped out in your mind, figure a route whereby you can circle the whole area. Pick a half-dozen landmarks to keep you on that route. If you will do just as I say you will, have no trouble." He paused for breath, then continued "Hell fires, you can cover that whole country in half a' day's ride. But first, you've got to know the lay of the land. Remember that son, that's good advice anytime, when you get confused, back up and get the lay of the land."

It was a much abused and picked-on twelve-year-old who rode out that morning, over Stot's hill, into the river bottoms, across the river and out onto the plateau where the sheep, were supposed to be. Sure enough, the butte (or 'nob' as Dad had called it) was there and it stood out plain and prominent above the surrounding hills. It looked like an awful waste of energy to climb it just to look around, but I had no choice.

Atop the butte, I staked my horse and plunked myself down. This was it! I would set right here all day and sulk. After all, it was his idea. He had said 'take all the time you want'. I would take all day. It is doubtful if many humans have probed the depths of gloom as deeply as I did that morning. Lucky for me I didn't have a can of worms or I would have eaten every one just so I would die and be a martyr to the cause of picked-on youngsters.

But smart as I was (or thought I was) there was one thing I didn't know, namely, that the hardest thing for any human, to do is nothing. I sat still a few minutes, then found Myself looking for ways to amuse myself. The panorama of hills and ravines and wilderness around me offered too great a challenge to my imagination and I found myself doing just what I had sworn not to do, studying and memorizing the details. Really, it was all quite simple. There were only three drainage basins and the land as far as I could see was all part of one big system. The hills and ravines which had confused me these last two days were just part of the network and, from my present vantage point, were not confusing at all.

Then the thought struck me (I hated to admit it) that I could circle the whole area in a few hour's ride. I could pick out some landmarks -- there were plenty to choose from—and I could cover every foot of ground before noon. Then I could return home and declare positively that so such thing as - a sheep herd existed in that part of the world.

My horse sensed a change of attitude and to grasp the idea that (from his point of view) there might be a way out of this, rat-race. He stepped out with a will and very shortly we arrived at landmark number one -- a lone pine tree. One down and five to go! Elated, I set course for number two -- an outcrop of red rock. There, I grinned triumphantly and spurred toward number three --- and rode smack-dab into a herd of sheep!

Joe was glad to see me. He read the letter, said "Hum-m-m!' and crumpled it in his pocket. Then he led me to his tent and a big dinner of lamb chops, and sour dough bread. Meanwhile he plied me with a thousand questions and talked, talked, talked

continuously. He was lonesome, and it was a treat for him to talk to someone, even a twelve-year-old kid.

The sun was still an hour high when I arrived home. Dad met me and asked, "Any luck" I ducked, my head and admitted "Yeah" He turned away but I'm sure I saw a sly grin on his face.

There are several reasons I mention this story. First, get the lay of the land. Understanding your audience is crucial to finding where your customers are. I've seen a business double their sales just by identifying their buyer personas. Personas are a good guess at who your customers are. But a lot can affect who is in your customer audiences, so they should be regularly re-evaluated. If you keep hammering the same target with your messaging, that audience will fatigue. Ad spend will increase, response rates will decrease, and your audience will begin to turn on you.

Developing personas should give you a lot of pain points that your segment is dealing with. A lot of times those pain points bleed over into other, untapped audiences. A great example is Nalgene water bottles. They were first created as bottles for laboratories. They were heat resistant, didn't react to harsh chemicals, and didn't break like glass. During the late 60's and early 70's, nature conservationists began discouraging the practice of burying or burning glass and aluminum cans in wilderness areas. Nalgene bottles were the perfect replacement. Built for durability and easily sealable. Nalgene seized upon the new market and spun off a new product line -- Nalgene Outdoor.

The second point I wanted to make with this story is that in order for your audiences to become aware of you; you have to meet them where they are.

It is more important for you to be aware of who these people are before they become aware of you. There are specific pain points that you have to speak to. They might have a set of vernaculars that you have to use when speaking to them. They also have interests and goals that are important for you to understand before you can start speaking to them.

These are often referred to as personas, profiles, avatars, customer groups. They are all the same thing.

There are a few things to remember with personas. They are not static. They don't represent your customers, and they can be a great tool to increase sales when used correctly. When used incorrectly, they are a fantastic way to pigeon hole your messaging and hobble future sales growth. Sometimes I don't know if a persona is the chicken, or the egg. In other words; is there a sales trend towards a market segment because we have been marketing to that group, or is the sales trend there because they resonate with the product?

I find personas useful because it identifies segments that have a pain point that you can solve with your product.

Let's suppose you sold kitchen knives. Any money that you spent advertising on Kids YouTube or Cartoon Network, won't give you very good returns. If you targeted people that are beginning culinary school, or engaged and newlywed couples, not only will you have to speak to each group differently, you will see a much better result when you do so.

In the Normal Life stage, there are 2 mental behaviors to be aware of:

Novelty

Self-sabotage

Novelty

In your mind, there are 2 conflicting scripts. One that seeks to maintain normalcy. Anything new is a potential threat and shouldn't be trusted until it has had a proving period. This script would love living in Phil's world in Groundhog Day. Everything is known. Threats are understood and predictable. Everything is awesome.

The conflicting script craves novelty. Boredom can actually stimulate parts of the brain that are active when you are in physical pain. To this script, boredom is the exact same thing as an injury.

In a study, participants were left in a room and given two choices. 1. They could either sit there and do nothing and be bored. 2. They could pass their time by shocking themselves. Many participants chose to shock themselves rather than deal with deal with boredom.

There are good reasons why we have both of these scripts. Anything that is unknown, and not within our realm of understanding is a huge threat to us. We don't know and can't predict the behavior of the new thing. What if the new neighbor is a sociopathic serial killer? What if that egg salad that someone brought to the potluck has been sitting out all day? What if I go on vacation to a foreign country and get kidnapped? These are all concerns brought up by this script. They aren't completely irrational fears.

Lack of understanding can be just as threatening. It is understanding that helps us predict behaviors in things around us. The better we can predict behavior, the safer something is. Curiosity also helps us discover new opportunities. We know that some mushrooms are edible, some are psychedelic, and some are poisonous, at some point, someone was curious enough to try them. I read a saying that I liked. It said "I'll bet the first person to try cow milk did lots of other crazy things"

It is important to know a little about the need to seek novelty in the normal state. This can be a powerful emotional motivator for someone who has their physical needs taken care of. In other words - affluent audiences.

Going back to the Maslow's Hierarchy of needs, people in this state are seeking and needing ways to build their esteem and achieve self-actualization. The higher up the scale of needs that a product or service helps someone achieve, the more expensive the product is.

As a marketer, it is a mistake to ignore or glaze over people in this segment because they are in the early stage of the story process.

The podcast Planet Money did a two-part series on buying a Birkin handbag. Birkin handbags are made by the French Luxury brand, Hermes. They have been the vogue bag to have for more than 30 years. The price tag for a Birkin - $60,000. The odd thing about a Birkin that Planet Money found was they are always out of stock.

Normally you would think that if you had a product that has that much markup, and you had a willing buyer, you would do all that you could to get the product in their hands as quickly as possible.

Birkin buyers can be on a waiting list to buy one of Hermes' bags for several years. Planet Money found a way to get around the waiting list is to already own a Birkin. They found someone that owned a Birkin, and when they brought that person along to stores that sold them, the stores mysteriously had a single Birkin in the store for sale.

So, why does Hermes put buyers through such a circus and a long waiting list? Purely for red rope effect. To create the perception of exclusivity. Owners of a Birkin bag have something that is novel and rare, which comes with a huge boost in social status.

Self-sabotage

Self-sabotage is the universal script that afflicts everyone. If you know how you self-sabotage, that's great. Knowing is half the battle. If you don't think that you self-sabotage, then you are in denial about your self-sabotage.

Self-sabotaging is anything you do to prevent yourself from accomplishing tasks or finding achievement. It is a conflict between what you can do and what you don't believe you can do.

Self-sabotage comes in a variety of forms:

Procrastination.

Self-medicating.

Self-injury or cutting.

Spending too much time watching TV or on social media when you have more important goals that you could be working on.

Letting fear talk you out of accomplishing something.

Worrying about something but not doing anything to fix it.

Blaming others and not taking responsibility for yourself

Having a negative view of the world

Letting trivial activities take priority over important goals

This is just a short list of just a few examples. The reason that I mention this is because… well, I have a few reasons. One is that in the normal, or status quo state of living, self-sabotage is showing up everywhere in a person's life. Whether that person recognizes it or not. The other reason I bring this up is because it might be affecting you right now. The third reason I bring this up is because self-sabotage originates from our old friend, the limbic system - our reptile brain.

Why does this occur? I don't know. I'm no psychologist. But I'll gladly toss my ideas out there. The reptile brain has a primary function for us; survival. As we be-bop through life, this part of our brain is peering out at the world around us. Sometimes it experiences traumatic events like being betrayed by a spouse, or hears a story - something like, you hear a friend talking about their uncle who won the lottery but immediately turned into a terrible, greedy person. Your reptile brain takes special note of those occurrences and puts up safety netting around those beliefs so that you don't accidentally stroll into that situation again.

Remember that the reptile brain doesn't have access to the portions of the brain that creates language. It communicates with feelings.

The next time you let someone get close to you, your reptile brain starts to make you feel extremely uncomfortable about your situation. Soon you are doing things to push that person away and non-consciously trying to destroy your relationship with that person. Your reptile brain is well intentioned. It really is.

In the normal state of life, there are plenty of opportunities for brands to lean into ways that people self-sabotage. It is a definite pain point that we all struggle with.

Agitation

When we talk about story writing, this is the agitation or the inciting incident before the call to adventure. This is where Happy Gilmore discovers his grandma's house is being foreclosed because she hasn't paid taxes for the past 10 years. This is when Dennis Nedry in Jurassic Park executes the command line to temporarily disarm the alarms while he sneaks out with his stolen dinosaur embryos.

In the marketing world, this is technically the awareness stage of the sales funnel. Sometimes we are aware of a problem. At the end of the day, you might notice white flakes of dead skin on your black shirt and realize you have dandruff. Other times, we don't realize there was a something to be concerned about until they are pointed out to us. A well-known example is the Crest white tissue test. Millions of people, (myself included) became aware that our teeth were hideously, and monstrously yellow. We saw a commercial that had a woman holding a tissue up next to her teeth and comparing the whiteness of her teeth to the whiteness of the tissue. If you've seen the ad, I'm certain that you've tried the tissue test. I'm also certain that your teeth were not as white as the tissue. And you realized you had a problem. Another example that I am very familiar with is a video that Purple created with the Harmon Brothers Agency. They shot dozens of intros to the video and tested which one performed the best. The version that had the best response rate was with Goldilocks standing in front of a bed. A text graphic appears. It says, "Goldilocks Bed Expert" and she says "What's a super easy way to tell that your bed is awful? The raw egg test!"

Up until the point in my life, I had never thought my bed might have been awful.

After Goldilocks captures your interest with an intriguing question, she demonstrates the raw egg test. In the next scene she is standing in front of a Purple mattress. A large pane of glass suspended over the bed that has 4 eggs glued to the bottom side. Goldilocks pulls on a release cord and the glass is dropped flat onto the mattress. As it impacts the mattress, the eggs are visibly not crushed under the weight of the glass.

Through the rest of the video, Goldilocks demonstrates the same test on all other types of mattresses. In each demonstration, the eggs are pulverized.

The goal of the agitation step is to make the reptile brain feel curious, uncomfortable or alert.

Kurt Vonnegut, who is a popular author recommended to other authors that they start as close to the end of the story as possible. A common technique used by writers in action and drama movies is to open their books or movie with an inciting incident. Star Wars opens right away with a battle scene and Princess Leia under attack. The Matrix begins with Trinity fighting her way out of a building.

Purple's best performing video intro started immediately with the inciting incident. They started as close to the end as possible.

You have one to two seconds to capture attention on landing pages and videos before your viewer is gone. Hook them with the inciting content.

How do you do that? The first thing to remember is that what we are doing in this first step is incite an emotional response. We are addressing the desires of the elephant. The elephant pays the most attention to 3 things:

Something that is either threatening, novel or pleasurable.

The rule of thumb to know which of these three strategies to use for your messaging is to ask yourself how your product or service solves the problems for your intended audience.

Consider the failed Pepsi ad. The video begins with Kendall Jenner at a photoshoot. A procession of protestors passes by in front of the location where she is. Kendall walks off the photo set and joins the protestors. Kendall wanders to the front of the group. There is a line of police officers blockading the protestors. Kendall breaks through the front of the line and strolls up to a policeman and hands him a Pepsi. This overwhelming act of generosity and goodwill removes all tension. The day is saved, thanks to Kendall and a single Pepsi. Pepsi immediately pulled the ad and took a huge backlash on social media for creating such a tone-deaf ad.

It's not very likely that a soft drink will solve your problems with something that is threatening. When Pepsi creates an ad that suggests a single can of Pepsi can solve social injustice and political unrest, it comes off as tone deaf. The only caveat that I can imagine in this guideline is when using humor. If the Pepsi ad were exaggerated and over-the-top, it might have been able to pull it off. But even then, the risk wouldn't have been worth the payout. Best to just stay in your lane with regards to how your product solves problems.

That also means that your messaging will change depending on the audience. This is because different issues are being addressed.

If I was marketing hot tubs to an audience segment of 18 - 25-year-old males. But, my ad jumped right into arthritis relief and spending time with grandkids. Or if my audience was 65-year olds that were retired. But, my ad looked like it was shot at a college frat party. Neither ad is going to perform well, and you will take some heat on social media.

How do you set up an inciting incident then? Lucky for us, Hollywood has already figured this out. No need to reinvent the wheel. This is by no means an all-inclusive list. I appreciate that there are hundreds of ways to slice and dice these.

Below are 5 ways that you could incite interest:

Inspirational

Before and after

Desire

Life altering

Intrigue

Inspirational

If your product solves a problem, prove it. Paint a vivid and sizzling picture of how life will be like after someone uses your product. Use as many senses as you can in your description. If they can't picture it, they won't buy it. Lead with a benefit. Use clear language. This isn't the time to be vague or use complicated vernacular.

As marketers we fall into a trap thinking that we have repeated the same message too many times. We assume that everyone else has heard a message as many times as we have. Inspirational messaging is one of the first things to go after we have been producing content after years. Sometimes even after a few months.

I've read several times that Einstein was a horrible professor. He had developed his intelligence so far beyond the point where he was an early student struggling to understand the concepts that he was now teaching. He had built so many layers on top of the information that he was teaching, that it all becomes compressed into one single gestural comment. I am sure he felt like everyone in class could keep up with what he was talking about because it seemed so simple to him.

Brands can do the same thing with their content strategies. Ironically, that is what made them successful. Think about the Rolling Stones. They formed 60 years ago. One of their most popular songs Paint it Black was released in 1966. That means for over 50 years, every time they got on stage, Mick Jagger had to belt out Paint it Black with as much conviction and energy as the first time he had played it. Do you think he's sick of that song? I would be.

I've thought the same thing about DJs that work

for an oldies station. I am sure DJs don't have to listen to songs they are playing on the radio anymore. Most of the song intros are pre-recorded in batches, so I don't think they are as sick of songs as much as Mick Jagger might be. But I still imagine a DJ sitting in a sound room with headphones on. He flips his mic on and says: "This is next one is coming at you all the way from 1966. One of my personal favorites! Good Vibrations from The Beach Boys!"
Then he Shuts his mic off. Rips the headphones off of his head as he hastily pours himself a shot from a whiskey bottle. The whiskey comes out of the bottle so fast, some of it sloshes onto the table. The DJ picks up the glass and chokes it down as he mutters "If I have to hear that song one more time… Why didn't I go into advertising like my sister did? At least she doesn't have to keep saying the same things about the same stuff for 50 years!" You are going to get sick of the things you keep saying. That doesn't mean your audience is tired of

it.

I am not saying that you shouldn't find new ways to say the same thing. It's important to refresh how you state your values and benefits.

The first example that comes to mind is the Old Spice The Man Your Man Could Smell Like Commercials. Every new commercial had the same underlying message. If you used Old Spice, you could be what women want their men to be like.

Before and after

Where the inspirational messaging talks only about the after, the before and after talks about both sides of the coin. Pretty obvious right? The power of this method is the contrast in situations. Terrible situations in the before situation, immediately contrasted with the euphoric post-purchase life. The better you can solidify your argument for your product, the more you are going to instigate that inner-elephant to start moving. Before and after is a compelling method to illustrate how your product benefits the user.

The Harmon Brothers Agency that created the Purple Goldilocks video, are masters of the before and after. Their videos are replete with excellent examples of before and after.

Let's take a look at a few of their ads.

The squatty potty pooping unicorn - 10 seconds into the video, the main character says "But you know who sucks at pooping? You do. That's because when you sit on the porcelain throne, this muscle puts a kink in the hose"

You are immediately presented with a problem that you didn't know you had. He continues "Is that a problem? I don't know? Are hemorrhoids a problem? Because sitting at this angle can cause hemorrhoids, bloating, constipation, and a buttload of other crap."

We are 45 seconds into the video and they have already spent the majority of the time painting a very uncomfortable image of your before life.

"But what happens when you go from a sit to a squat? Voila! And the muscle relaxes, and that kink goes away faster than a Pegasus laying a sweet sherbet dookie."

And there you have it. A simple explanation of your life after using a squatty potty. No more hemorrhoids. No more bloating. No more constipation.

Let's move on to another one of their videos, Chatbooks.

The video starts with a smiling woman in a bath surrounded by bubbles. Candles flickering around her. She says "I have three kids and I work from home, so people always ask me how I stay so calm and organized. I have three kids and I work from home, so people always ask me how I stay so calm and organized.

I'm kidding! Do you think I have time for a bath? I'm fully clothed, I fell in the tub while I was timing my son holding his breath." She stands up and is soaking wet in her clothes. Her son stands up. He is wearing goggles and swimming trunks. "26 seconds! Now go fetch mommy's hairdryer. Motherhood goes by too fast. I haven't slept more than 4 hours in 12 years! My diet consists of the protein bars and pita chips I inhale in the dark in my pantry, and my children are growing like weeds, but I barely have enough time to keep them alive, let alone print pictures of them. Because here's the problem, what the fork? Making photo books sucks!"

They took a bit longer to get to the main problem, but look how well it illustrates the before? Once again, any parent, or even busy person can relate to this. We have an extremely vivid understanding of the problem that a minute ago, you didn't even realize you had. Now you understand that you are too busy. Life is passing you by. Your memories are not getting captured. Your elephant now has FOMO (Fear of missing out) and you have a limited resource of time that might be getting wasted. What are you supposed to do?

The video keeps going almost non-stop from the first second until 1:30 into the video filling in the image of your before life.

"Don't get me wrong, I love Instagram, but my kids never see our photos, they refuse to follow me. Hi Jeffrey, you're doing great! But now there's a solution I do have time for because it takes no time. Introducing Chatbooks, the app that automatically creates quality photo books from your phone. Chatbooks is shockingly easy, because you already did the work when you took the photos. Chatbooks creates and ships a photo book to you every time you add 60 photos to Instagram, Facebook, or your phone favorites. It even includes the original dates and captions. It's like getting a magazine subscription to your own life… Plus, these Chatbooks cost just $8, that's what you'd pay for a day's worth of diapers, except you fill Chatbooks with the kind of crap you care about."

The other benefit of before and after is that you

can't pull it off without using elements of story. The before and after is really just a very short and succinct hero's journey.

Desire

Creating desire for your product or service is kind of the point of this whole book. Desire is born out of your inner-elephant wanting to move in the direction of something. Sometimes, if the elephant rider is unbiased about that desire, the elephant can move to that desire without any friction. If you were craving a salad that you saved for lunch, and it was lunchtime, and it was a healthy salad; your frontal cortex doesn't have any objections to you having that salad.

If you supply the elephant rider with logical reasons (product features) to move in the same direction as the elephant, then you've created desire. At that point, the only obstacles are external. Teslas are one of the fastest production cars being produced. My inner-elephant wants a

Tesla. You never have to fill them up with expensive gas. I could save a lot on fuel costs if I owned a Tesla. That appeals to my logical frontal cortex. My rider wants a Tesla. Why don't I own a Tesla? I don't have $120,000 for the Tesla that I want. That's a huge external friction point for me.

Life altering

I suppose you could make the argument that anything is life altering if you pull at your emotional appeals. I have a favorite commercial to watch. It begins with a rapid succession of high-speed camera shots of a Dodge Aries car. Lots of blurred motion graphics with a soundtrack of an upbeat guitar/techno beat in the background. Then a man appears on screen. He's sitting and looking sideways at the camera. It all has a very conversational feel to it.

"Hi, I'm Tim. I drive an Aries!" He says at the camera.

More fast shots of the car.

"I think the typical Aries driver is changing for the better!" he continues as he nods his head.

A text graphic fades in that says "The '88 Aries beat the '87 Hyundai pony in 3 out of 4 comparison road tests"

Tim continues "I like the cool stuff!"

Text graphics fade in and out that say "Booya", "22HP engine… standard", "Bench seat… standard', "2 speaker radio now in FM… standard", "Map light… standard"

Tim is back again "It's not only the performance, it's the luxury!"

Text graphic fades in that says "Over 85% of Aries owners have a fixed address"

The final outro says "Dodge Aries. $200 or best offer" and it has Tim's number on it.

Tim almost makes an '88 Dodge Aries sound like it might change my life… Almost.

The important part about using life altering statements to create interest in your product is that they need to be plausible and believable. The ordinary life of your customer is in reality. If you are going to stake a flag in the territory of life altering, everyone assumes that this is a positive change and it is a dramatic change.

I am sure that buying a ream of paper is life altering. You might use that paper to print out a resume that gets you a fantastic job that changes your life. (If you work somewhere that sells paper like Dunder Mifflin, feel free to steal that idea.) But the connection to that life changing event isn't as solid as something like a weight loss program.

Intrigue

The last technique I wanted to mention to create interest is intrigue. In the intrigue step, we are capturing the interest of the inner-elephant. That can be with a bit of fear, curiosity, delight, humor, or even a sense of belonging.

That's great, but how? The easiest way to create intrigue is to leverage your unique selling proposition (USP), your secret sauce, your unique identifier. If you don't have any differentiators from you and your competitors, you've got a lot more problems than this book helps you with. I don't know, you might as well go do something different with your life, because you aren't going to last much longer in your current business. Your product doesn't have ANY differentiators? Oh, it has a green bottle and your competition has a blue bottle? Why didn't you say so? OK, so you DO have something unique. Next time just tell me that so that we don't have to have this discussion again, mmmkay?

What we are trying to do here is get the inner elephant up and paying attention to you are doing, and ready for information on which way to go. We do this by presenting the problem, or a hint at the problem but not giving clues to where the solution is. But **spoiler alert! ** the answer to the problem is always your USP.

84 Lumber created an ad with the agency Brunner that aired during Super Bowl 51. It was a 90

second ad (A long and expensive ad for the Super Bowl). It portrayed a young Mexican girl and her mother (remember how we talked about creating empathy for your main character? Another example here) who are waking up early, saying goodbye to their family and beginning their journey to America through the desert. It created so much intrigue, the website visitors crashed the 84 Lumber website after it aired.

In the full version of the film, the two reach the border and discover a long wall extending the length of the border stopping them from crossing. After a sullen gaze at the wall, they notice a door in the wall, presumably made out of wood from 84lumber.com. They push on the door and cross safely into America.

84 Lumber claimed that the ad was not meant to be political, it still caused a lot of confusion and discussion about what it was supposed to be about. Not the best example to use, but this still illustrates how an intriguing ad might work to generate

interest.

I go back to my original statement about creating intrigue. Present a problem that is answered by your USP. If 84 Lumber had stayed closer to a topic that was answered by their USP, they would have fared much better.

Meet the Mentor

Most, if not all stories have meet the mentor moment. The main character is pulled out of their ordinary life. They take up the call to action and before they encounter the big ordeal, they meet a mentor that gives them the tools, information, and confidence they will need to overcome their upcoming challenge.

This is your Yoda, Gandolf, Jiminy Cricket, Dumbledore, Mr. Miyagi, Mufasa, and Professor X.

In the marketing sense, the mentor is your product or service. It is such an easy pit to fall into when we are talking about our own brands to assume that our product is the hero.

I'm not saying it isn't easy to think that way. Our customer has problem X. Our product fixes that problem. Sounds a lot like a hero to me, right? Take a look at the scenario from your customer's point of view. When we tell someone that we are going to come in and take control of the situation and solve the problem, they have to step aside and let us take care of it. What the inner-elephant hears is: you won't have control over the situation. My product is more important than you are. I don't think you have value. To the limbic system, that is interpreted as a threat. The frontal cortex might very well be on board with what you are saying. Everything checks out logically, but the ol' emotion control center is trying everything it can to backpedal out of the deal.

Brands who find themselves in a situation where there are rampant cancellations, returns, and/or excessive negative reviews, it is always a hero complex situation.

I pulled a services description off completely random carpet cleaner's website. It says:

Any of our three skilled and knowledgable cleaning techs will provide a thorough cleaning of your carpet, tile, and upholstery restoring it to look great again.

Where do I start with this one? Three words into this website and they've already said "our". And, three cleaning technicians? That actually sounds like a small business. I'm concerned that if I do call their number, it will be disconnected because they've already gone out of business.

7 words in and there's a party foul typo? It should be knowledgeable, not knowlegable.

"Cleaning techs" - industry jargon. I haven't finished the first sentence on their website and I'm already feeling a bit squeamish about their services.

I finally got through the first sentence and got to "restoring it to look great again". Hey! That's like a half benefit… I think? Good job guys!

Moving on.

We treat your home and property as if it were our own by using furniture foot protectors, shoe covers, and wall guards.

First word is "We" = :(

After reading the whole sentence, my mind was planted with a worry about their service that I hadn't even imagined before I got here. Having my carpets cleaned can actually result in damage to my furniture, tracked in dirt, and scuffed up walls? Thanks! Now I'm not only less compelled to call, I have one more apprehension about industry as a whole that I hadn't even considered. It's better to replace my carpet rather than clean them? It's starting to sound safer and smarter?

Next.

State of the Art Equipment

Our high power, high temperature truck mount cleaning units are simply the best available. A higher temp cleaning means a cleaner carpet and a happier customer. We use soft water for all our cleaning. Soft water leaves the carpet feeling soft and fluffy not crunchy like hard water leaves it. First word again, is "Our". Uh, "high power, high temperature" I don't know, is that a good thing? It must be if you are bragging about it. "Truck mount cleaning units"? The only people that know what that means is you and your three cleaning techs. "A higher temp cleaning means a cleaner carpet and a happier customer." Oh… you are talking me? If I haven't bailed by now, and I called to have my carpets cleaned by one of your skilled and knowledgeable (but not very literate) cleaning techs, me -- being the customer would be "happier" because you used what you are referring to as a "higher temp"? Good job! You might have stumbled upon another half benefit to using your service.

Now wait a minute! The next sentence I'm learning about soft water. It… it leaves my carpet "soft and fluffy". I would love soft and fluffy carpet not that crunchy carpet that hard water leaves. Ew, yuck! Hard water, why you gotta be so nasty all the time? I don't know what soft water is, but I'm a soft water fan boy for life now. 2 benefits in 2 sentences. We are on a roll here. I'm excited to see what the next description brings!

Environmentally Safe

Low VOC detergents along with a thorough rinsing process will satisfy those who want a cleaning that will be healthier not only for their family, but healthier for the earth.

"Low VOC detergents", "Satisfy those who want a cleaning" Are we... are we still talking about carpets? Because it sounds like... well, I don't know what you are talking about here. But now I'm worried about more things if I get my carpets cleaned. I could hurt my family and the environment?

Nah! I'm good. Second thought, I don't need my carpets cleaned. I'll learn to ignore how disgusting they look. It's not worth the risk to my home, my family and the environment.

Let's see what we can do here to help our carpet cleaners out.

Let's take their potential customers through the first 3 stages of the hero's journey and see if it sounds better. First, Normal life, which we can actually roll up into the agitate step if we use a before and after. Then we'll move them on to meet the mentor -- our carpet cleaners, who are here to help the customer save the day.

Dear homeowner,

I don't know if you remember me, but it is me, your carpet. I know you've been pretty busy lately, always running off to this or that. I wish I could go places and see things.

Sometimes you take a shower before you leave. That must feel amazing! ...being clean.

So, I don't know if you noticed or not, but I got a new stain the other day. It kind of blends in with the other stains, and grungy traffic patterns. I'm stained everywhere now.

Remember when you and I used to snuggle up together? You'd be reading a book, watching TV, or staring out the window while daydreaming? Sometimes you would run your hand over my fibers back when they were soft and fluffy. Now, nobody wants to use me because I'm crusty and gross.

You used to be so proud of me too! People used to walk in and ask why your house smelled so good. You would proudly point to me and say, "It's because my nice, clean carpets." and people would remark how beautiful I was. I used to be so beautiful. You were so much happier back then.

Did you know that XYZ Carpet Cleaners are experts at rolling back the clock on carpets like me? They can gently clean me with environmentally safe detergents that leave me looking fresh, clean, and snuggly soft. You'll be proud of me again. You can curl up on me under your favorite blanket again. You will be so much happier like you used to be when we were together.

Call XYZ Carpet Cleaners (123) 456-8910 Have marvelously clean carpets again.

That's obviously a very copy-heavy description. The higher a prospect is in the sales funnel, the more copy it will take to persuade them. Still, this is a rough draft. I would pare it down more than this. Run some A/B testing. Who knows-- a simple "Make your carpets clean again" might outperform this.

There're a few commercials that are great at illustrating the concept of meet the mentor. My favorite is the "You're Not You When You're Hungry" Snickers ad. The first one that I saw began with a bunch of men playing backyard football. In the middle of a play Betty White appears, slowly shuffling down field. Someone appears from out of the screen running full speed at Betty as the ball is thrown to her. She takes a brutal hit and lands in a mud puddle. In the next clip, everyone is standing around in the huddle. Someone says to Betty, "Mike, what's wrong with you? You are playing like Betty White!" Betty shoots back at him "That's not what your girlfriend said!" Their banter is interrupted by a woman running up to the huddle from the sideline yelling "Hold on guys!" She hands Betty a Snickers and says, "Eat this." Betty incredulously asks "Why?" The woman responds, "Because you're not you when You're hungry." Betty takes a bite and the woman asks "Better?" Suddenly Betty is gone and there is a man standing there that we now realize is Mike. He says "Better!"

That is a great meet the mentor moment. It's also a good before and after example. Which brings up a good point; each step of the hero's journey doesn't need to have its own dedicated step. You can roll steps up into one sequence. You can even skip steps. There's no hard-fast rule that says you have to adhere to each step. Movies do it all the time. Marketers can skip steps in the sales funnel without losing conversions. It makes it easier to skip steps if you know what you are doing and what the risks are.

The Ordeal

In a movie, this is what you would think of when the movie hits the climax. This is the scene where Rocky fights Apollo. The scene where Marv and Harry attempt to break into Kevin's house in Home Alone. The moment in The Matrix when Neo enters back into the matrix to save Morpheus. It's the whole reason we are watching the movie. It's the part where we are sitting on the edge of our seats waiting to see what happens next.

In terms of the sales funnel, it is the purchase. It's the whole reason that we shop. Fairly straight forward step.

For the elephant and the rider; at this step our little

elephant gets a little reward. Technically, the elephant rewards the rider. The limbic system will produce dopamine whenever it experiences something new, or something good. We have dopamine receptors that receive the dopamine and the result is a small rush of euphoria and a good feeling.

For marketers, this is the point of the story, where the credits roll up the screen. The movie is over. Another successful purchase. High fives all around!

For the customer, our hero in this story, they still have to journey back to their regular life, having conquered the dragon and found the elixir. If we fall out of their story at this point, we miss the opportunity develop brand loyalists, gain referrals, and help overcome concern, so that they don't enter the desolate, dreary, and lonely lands of Buyer's Remorse.

Several things can go wrong in the minds of our customers after purchase. Emotionally, a customer might feel alienated. Experience group exclusion rather than anticipated inclusion. They can also feel like the anticipated benefits don't match up with the actual experienced benefits, which can make them feel tricked and disrespected. Let me tell you something, inner-elephants dislike being disrespected. They hates it.

The rider can sometimes notice a chasm between promised features and realized features. If you bought a speaker and you thought it was wireless, but after purchasing it, you realized that it had to be plugged into an outlet. You are going to return it… maybe. What if you listened to the speaker and realized that it actually sounded great. Then a group of your friends heard the speaker. They made a big deal about how great it sounded and praised you for being able pick such high quality audio equipment. You might let the fact that it isn't battery powered slide just a little bit. In other words, if your inner-elephant still sees benefits, unless it is a huge objection by the rider, the elephant will get its way.

To help your customer along their story line, post-purchase is the perfect time to affirm that your customer has made the correct decision. Include in packaging, and follow-up communications, testimonials from previous customers talking about how they were able to use their product to overcome a challenge in their life, or how much they love their purchase.

If you have any sort of user groups, customer organizations, insider clubs, or memberships, post-purchase is when you want to get your customer introduced to those groups. We are wired to search out groups to be included in. We associate that with protection and safety.

During the purchase process you should be thinking about optimizing upsells, cross-sells, down-sells. I don't know if it's me, but when I hear marketers talk about upsells and cross-sells, and down-sells, I immediately picture a used car salesman huckster that is trying to sell you a termite protection plan to go along with that rust-bucket Buick you are trying to talk the price down on. I'm not talking about that. We've already established that if your products and services are not serving a purpose to your customer, then you either need to figure out what the benefits are, or you won't be in business long. Your upsells need to compliment the purchase or also solve the same problem your customer is experiencing. Simple as that.

The Rebirth

Neo has just rescued Morpheus and is trying to get out of the matrix. Meanwhile, sentinels are attacking the ship, the Nebuchadnezzar, where Neo's body is outside of the matrix. Tank tells Neo to run to room 303. Agent smith is right on Neo's heels. Neo kicks open the door to room 303. Inside, Agent Smith awaits with a gun. He shoots Neo point blank. Agent Smith checks Neo to make sure he is dead. In the Nebuchadnezzar the Sentinels have entered and are cutting through the ship.
Trinity is leaning over Neo's body and whispers "Neo, I'm not afraid anymore. The Oracle told me

that I would fall in love and that man... the man that I loved would be the One. So, you see, you can't be dead. You can't be... because I love you. You hear me? I love you." As she kisses him, he suddenly gasps in a breath of air.

In the matrix, Neo opens his eyes. Trinity orders Neo "Now get up!"

When the agents see Neo stand back up, the unload their guns on him. Neo calmly raises his hands and stops the bullets in mid-air.

"What's happening?" asks Tank. "He is the One," says Morpheus.

Agent Smith runs at Neo and tries to attack him. Neo blocks Agent Smith's punches and kicks Agent Smith against the wall. To Agent Smith's horror, Neo appropriates into Agent Smith's body causing it to explode into bits of matrix code. Agents Brown and Jones look at each other and run away in fear.

Textbook example of a rebirth in a story. Post-purchase should be the time that you are most available and attentive through customer service channels. Most customers cost you a lot of money to acquire. All it takes is one bad experience for that person to tell their friends and family about their story. Suddenly you have a cell of brand haters. On the flip side, a positive customer experience can flip them on to be a huge brand advocate.

As a side gig, I used to repair phone and tablet screens. I had a woman bring me an iPad with a broken screen. The day after I repaired it for her, she sent me a message saying that she didn't know what had happened. The screen on the iPad had cracked again. I had charged her $80 for the repair. Because it was a newer model, the parts were still pretty high. The screen on hers cost me $40. I knew if I told her that I would repair it again at no charge, I would be breaking even and taking a wash on the labor. My first thought was to charge her an extra $20. But I was having a hard time sourcing quality parts for the newer iPads. Every time I found a supplier that would send me a good screen, inevitably their quality would start slipping. I had no way of telling if she had dropped the iPad again and was upset because she had just paid to have it repaired. Or if it was a poor-quality screen and had fractured from the stresses of being adhered to an iPad. Reluctantly, I told her to bring it back and I would put a new screen on for her at no cost. When she picked it up, she didn't seem to be particularly excited or upset with me about the whole situation. Everything seemed normal to me. About an hour after she left, my phone blew up with notifications. She went home and posted a message about me on one of the biggest Facebook group garage sale pages in the area. She said that I had fixed her iPad, it had mysteriously broken the next day. But, I had promptly fixed it again at no cost, and she recommended my repair services to anyone. A positive review.

I had never experienced the benefits of a positive review like that. INSANE! You ever see a zombie movie and a character sees a zombie coming, they turn, there's another zombie! Turn around, there's more! Instantly they are surrounded? I felt like that, except they weren't zombies. They were people with wads of money and broken electronics in their hand, wanting me to fix their phones and tablets. It was fantastic! I even had professional athletes contacting me from France to fix their phones based off of that one review.

That is what gave me enough confidence to quit my day job to fix electronics full-time. I then proceed to fail miserably. I gained key life experiences and the impetus to begin writing this book.

Post-purchase experiences will either make or break a company. Most business models barely break even on a customer acquisition. Lots of companies take a loss on the initial purchase. Why are you wasting your time and money with new acquisitions? No, ya dummy. The money is in the banana stand.

It is all about the customer journey AFTER the purchase. The lifetime value of the customer. The good news is that if you stick the landing on the post-purchase experience, repeat purchases, and customer referrals will happen by themselves.

The Return with the Elixir

At the end of Moana; Moana places the heart of Te Ka back in the spiral on Te Ka's chest. This transforms Te Ka into Te Fiti, the lush and green island that she once was. As a reward, Te Fiti gives Moana a new boat and gives Maui a new fish hook.

Moana sails back to her island of Motonui where the flowers and fruit are blossoming. Her parents and her people greet her. The ocean gives her a pink seashell that she places on the sacred mountain. She takes her people sailing and teaches them to voyage on the seas like they used to. Her grandmother as a spirit guide manta ray directs them through the ocean.

The Return with the Elixir step is where the story wraps up. The hero returns to normal life having changed from their experiences. The villain receives a punishment that is befitting to their crime. The questions that were raised during the story are wrapped up.

In the sales funnel, this is referral programs, reviews and rewards programs.

The reptile brain feels safe in numbers, wants to feel inclusion, and craves respect and admiration from others. After using your product or service it is the best time to introduce these programs to your customer. Not only will it decrease returns and complaints, it will increase the lifetime value of customers. They will repeat purchase. You will grow by word of mouth, which is a much cheaper customer acquisition tool. And your customers will be avid brand loyalists.

When a customer starts telling people about the benefits of your product, when they start telling your story, it becomes their story. Your product becomes part of who they are. I had a coworker that went to school with a woman that had the dashboard of a Pontiac Trans-am tattooed on her arm. One day he asked her about her tattoo. She said "It's not a car. It's a lifestyle!"

It's not very often that Pontiac develops a follower like that. But think about some of the mega-brands: Apple, Nike, Amazon, Google. You and I wouldn't think twice if we saw an Apple or Nike logo tattooed on someone. So, do brands become popular because they did a great job of telling a story? Or did they become part of people's stories because they were popular? If you've read any part of this book, you'd realize that I'd say it is the brands that were great at intertwining their story with their customer's story.

TLDR

As I have used these steps in the hero's journey, I found it sometimes difficult to remember where in the sales funnel the customer was. And what type of messaging is best to move them to the next step. I found it helpful to create a reference chart for quick reference.

Customer Journey Stage	Compelling Motivators to the next step
Normal Life	Pain points, discomfort, Annoyances, boredom
Agitation	Benefits first followed by features.
Meet the Mentor	Obtain resolution to pain points mentioned in step 1
The Ordeal	Purchase the product/service
Rebirth	Return to normalcy having changed
Return with the Elixir	Share their discoveries and knowledge with others

www.ingramcontent.com/pod-product-compliance
Lightning Source LLC
Chambersburg PA
CBHW071537220526
45469CB00003B/821